Volume II in a series
"Narrow Gauge Railways of Europ

THE RAILWAYS
AND TRAMWAYS OF MAJORCA

by

Giles Barnabe

Plateway Press , P.O. Box 973, Brighton, BN2 2TG
ISBN 1 871890 13 5

ACKNOWLEDGEMENTS

In preparing a work of this nature the author has inevitably relied on the knowledge and memory of a great number of people, who so kindly supplied information, excerpts from old magazine articles, timetables, photographs, or spent time digging into various archives. A major tribute is due to a fellow narrow gauge enthusiast, the late David Lloyd, whose enquiry in the pages of Continental Modeller for information on the FC de Soller helped start the whole project.

I should particularly like to thank the Editors of Continental Modeller and Scale Model Trains for permission to re-use some previously published scale drawings, and also the following for their patience and help:- Celso Calvino Andreu, Michael Andress, John H. Buehler, Kenneth Dobeson, Anthony Fairclough, Andrew Harris, Andy Hart, Jordi Ibanez, Lawrence Marshall, F. Santiago Marques (Transports de Palma), Pedro de Montaner, Geoff Moore, Jaime Arrom Morla, Matias Mut, Andrew Neale, J.B. Nisbet, H.L. Norman, D. Palmer, Miss J. Patry, K.P.Plant, J.H.Price, Jorge Rabell, Trevor Rowe, Don Sibley, F.M. Simpson, Mike Swift, Keith Taylorson, Mike Tebbett, George Toms, John K. Williams, Jeremy Wiseman, Conselleria de Treball y Transports (Palma), Babcock & Wilcox Española S.A., Krupp Maschinentechnik GmbH, Orenstein & Koppel.

Disclaimer:- Exploring railways, whether they are in use or derelict, can have its dangers and every care should be taken. The description of locations in this book does not imply the right of public access and the writer and publisher can take no responsibility for any mishaps, however caused, to readers visiting the Majorcan railways.

© Giles Barnabe / Plateway Press 1993

Printed in Great Britain by Wayzgoose PLC, East Road, Sleaford, Lincs.

ISBN 1 871890 13 5

Scale drawings, maps and diagrams are by the Author.
Cover Artwork by John Holroyde.
Book Design by Keith Taylorson / Martin Snow - Intersoft Multimedia.

Front cover illustration: the Palma roundhouse of the FC de Mallorca, pictured in 1955, with Nasmyth Wilson 4-6-0T ALGAIDA (right) awaiting the call of duty. (B.A.Butt)
(Inset) A 1958 scene on the 3ft. gauge Palma Tramway system. Car No. 29 leaves Plaza San Antonio for Soledad. (Jeremy Wiseman)

Back cover: Entrance to the Ferrocaril de Soller station at Palma. (Author)

Frontispiece: On the FC de Mallorca, MTM No. 19 LLUCHMAYOR and a Babcock 2-6-2T make a rousing start from Palma with a heavy train on 27th February 1955. (B.A. Butt)

CONTENTS

		Page
Foreword		4

Part One: The FC de Mallorca

Chapter 1	The Birth of the Railway	5
Chapter 2	A History of the Line	9
Chapter 3	Locomotives and Other Motive Power	23
Chapter 4	Rolling Stock	33
Chapter 5	The Route Described	39
Chapter 6	Timetables and Train Working	67

Part Two: The FC de Soller

Chapter 7	A History of the Soller Railway	77
Chapter 8	Locomotives and Rolling Stock	83
Chapter 9	The Soller Line Described	89

Part Three: Other Lines

| Chapter 10 | Independent Railways and Tramways of Majorca | 97 |

Annexe	Other Balearic Railways	106
Appendix I	A list of Majorca Railway locomotives/railcars	107
Appendix II	Table of locomotive dimensions	110
Appendix III	Timetables of the Majorca Railway	112
Appendix IV	The Soller Railway Rule-book	118

| Bibliography | | 120 |

| Scale Drawings | | 121 |

FOREWORD

My first glimpse of the FC de Mallorca (Majorca Railways) was from a bus travelling to a holiday hotel in Porto Cristo in the early 1970s. Unfortunately that visit provided no further opportunity to follow up this tantalising sighting, and for some years I forgot all about Majorca's railway. Then in 1981 there came the opportunity to return to the island, where I discovered a narrow gauge railway system whose working parts were in the throes of a violent modernisation programme. Set against this however were many fascinating kilometres of derelict track where, with only a little imagination, the clock could be turned back thirty years or more - it must be added that these areas were well away from the usual tourist haunts. At station after station the railway appeared to be merely asleep rather than closed and, weeds apart, one could almost imagine that a train would arrive sometime later in the day. However the reality was that in much of the island the locals had forgotten their railway link with Palma in favour of road transport. Over on the north side of the island the FC de Soller was still in business, with equipment that had been in continuous use for over fifty years, thus providing a rare view of a past era of transport. The aged trains were obviously popular with the visitors as the services were well patronised.

A further visit to the island was undertaken in 1984. In the time since my previous visit the dereliction of the FC de Mallorca seemed to have accelerated and it was obvious that time was running out for some parts of the system. The task of recording as much as possible of the railway therefore took on an added urgency, and details of track layouts, buildings and rolling stock were sketched and photographed.

Other changes were taking place. Since my first visit the emphasis on the use of Castillian Spanish had given way to a resurgence of the local dialect, Mallorquin. This has resulted in changes to some of the local place names. For the purposes of this book I have retained, wherever possible, the names in use when the railway was built, using as my sources the original timetables or the names that are carved on the station walls themselves. I hope that readers in the Balearic Islands who favour the new spelling will forgive me.

What of the future? The FC de Soller looks secure although with the expiry of the railway company's concession in 2003, when the line reverts to State control, one might forsee changes possibly including rationalisation of the trackwork to metre gauge or replacement of the rolling stock in daily use. It is to be hoped that the elegant electric motor coaches and the wooden carriages will be retained at least for the popular Tourist Specials, but this might prove difficult should the electrical infrastructure need major renovation some time in the future. If such an occurrence were to place an intolerable financial burden on the line's management one could see the real possibility of a policy of dieselisation being implemented, and much of the railway's present charm being swept away.

On the neighbouring FC de Mallorca it appears that the nationalised remains of the line have a future, if only between Palma and Inca. Elsewhere other parts of FEVE are being handed over to the control of local provincial authorities, and it is interesting to speculate what effects this might have on the FC de Mallorca; possibly some of the earlier expansion plans might be revived in order to save road congestion during the summer months. Faint rumours have reached the writer of a preservation movement to buy up a section of abandoned line and run steam-hauled tourist trains using preserved locomotives brought in from industrial or other defunct lines on the mainland. Unfortunately no confirmation of this scheme appears to be forthcoming. If the writer had a dream it would be of seeing steam trains running on some of these tracks again. The section from Arta to Manacor is situated near the resorts on the east coast, and is not too far distant from the holiday conurbations round the Bay of Palma, so there is certainly a traffic potential. The centre of the island enjoys pleasantly wild scenery and with only one or two exceptions the old level crossings on this section occur on minor country roads where inconvenience to road traffic would be minimal. Who knows, perhaps the FC de Mallorca may one day awake to a renewed future. Let us hope so.

Giles Barnabe
London, 1992.

PART ONE: THE MAJORCA RAILWAY

Chapter 1
The Birth Of The Railway

To set the scene for the dawn of Majorca's "Railway Age" one must forget all tourist pre-conceptions of the island today. In the mid-nineteenth century the island was still a poor and rather isolated province of Spain, though some earlier restrictive trading laws were being eased, leading to a wider contact with the outside world. Luckily a clear picture of contemporary local life has been left by Charles Bidwell, the British Consul who witnessed the inauguration of the Majorca Railway, which he described in his book "The Balearic Islands", published in 1876. At that time the island's economy was predominantly agricultural and primitive, while industry was mostly carried out at home or in small workshops in the Palma area, using cheap labour. As well as rice and olive oil, shoe-making and soap manufacture provided important exports. About a quarter of the inhabitants lived in the capital, while the remainder were spread through the island's towns and villages. Travel depended on animal power and the roads were poor dirt tracks, a round trip of some twenty kilometres being the most that could be accomplished in one day. The Sierra de Alfabia mountains cut off the northern coastline which was best reached by sea from Palma.

The idea of a Majorcan railway was first mooted as early as 1852 when an Iron Road was proposed to link Palma and Inca, but this scheme never progressed beyond the discussion stage. Four years later a more serious attempt was made when a Belgian engineer, Paul Bouvy, presented a study for a broad gauge line to link Palma and Inca with a branch line from Santa Maria to Porreras, while a second branch would link Montuiri and Manacor. At about the same time two Catalan engineers, the Gispert brothers, proposed a different route between Palma and Inca, and as this scheme promised a quick return for the investors' capital, money was quickly subscribed, possibly at the expense of Bouvy's scheme which appears not to have progressed beyond the prospectus stage. For some reason the Gisperts' original plan also seems to have met with unexpected difficulties as shortly afterwards the brothers presented another scheme for Government approval. This time a more ambitious plan was outlined:- the main line was to take a roundabout route northwards from Palma to Bunyola before heading south-east to serve Santa Maria; it would then run north-east as far as Inca, finally swinging round to the north by way of Llubi and La Puebla to reach Alcudia. From Santa Maria a branch line was to run south-east to Porreras before heading up towards Manacor. Although government funding for these plans was granted in 1864, the political upheavals leading to the revolution of 1868 meant that the plan was never implemented.

The quest for a successful Majorcan railway project was once again taken up when in 1871 another local engineer, Eusebio Estado, produced a study examining the island's commerce and the benefits of linking Palma and Inca by rail; his route was similar to Bouvy's, but this time the gauge was to be 3ft in order to save expense. The following year, in 1872, The Majorca Railway Company was formed to open the line which was to be some eighteen miles long. All the necessary capital was subscribed locally, in total amounting to 8,500,000 Reals (or £88,000 at the contemporary exchange rates). The sum was raised in shares of 2,000 Reals and the line was probably the only Spanish provincial railway to be built without foreign capital.

By this time several narrow gauge lines had been built in Spain, those promoted by British concerns having gauges varying between 3ft 6ins and 4 ft, while Spanish-backed narrow gauge lines mostly favoured a gauge of one metre (which after the passing of the Law of Secondary and Economic Railways in 1904 became the mandatory Spanish narrow gauge for all new lines). Why, then, was the Majorca Railway built to a gauge of 3ft? The fact that the original material was obtained from Britain where the 3ft gauge was rapidly becoming the "standard" narrow gauge may explain matters. Others have theorised that a cancelled rolling stock order, intended for a British colony, was diverted to Majorca and thus made the choice for the Majorcan engineer - though this explanation savours somewhat of the tail wagging the dog and is made less likely by the negotiations

EARLY RAILWAY PROPOSALS

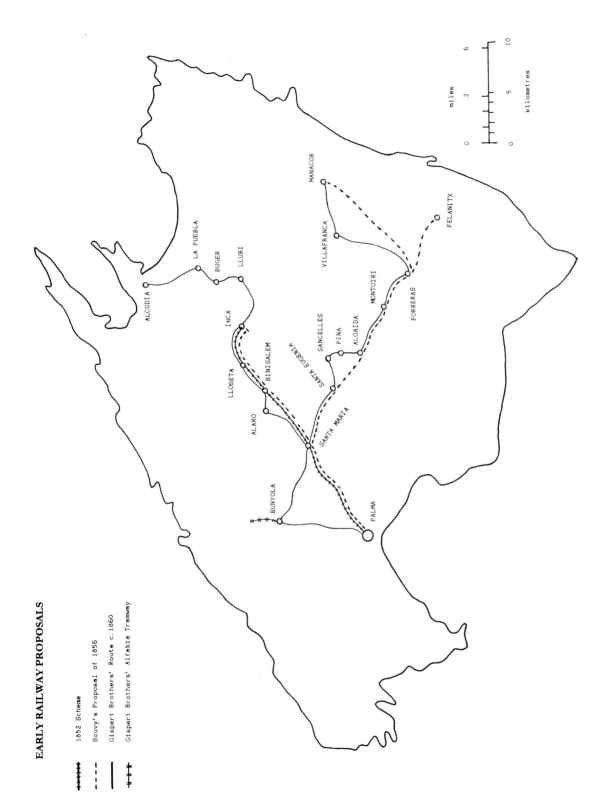

┼┼┼┼┼   1852 Scheme

- - - -   Bouvy's Proposal of 1856

———   Gispert Brothers' Route c.1860

╫╫╫╫   Gispert Brothers' Alfabia Tramway

ALCUDIA

LA PUEBLA

BUGER

LLUBI

INCA

LLOSETA

BINISALEM

ALARO

SANTA EUGENIA

SANCELLES

PINA

ALGAIDA

MONTUIRI

SANTA MARIA

BUNYOLA

PALMA

MANACOR

VILLAFRANCA

FELANITX

PORRERAS

miles

kilometres

0   5   10

0   3   6

carried out between the railway company and various British suppliers of rolling stock. From the evidence of the signatures on various Brown Marshall rolling stock plans it appears that Eusebio Estado and a collegue, Antonio Ankerman, visited Britain during 1873 and placed orders for the equipment needed to open the railway.

Construction of the line to Inca went ahead with few difficulties as there were no real natural obstacles to overcome. The ruling gradient was 1 in 72, with the sharpest curve set at a radius of 17.4 chains. The original rails were supplied in 10 metre lengths and weighed 20kg/metre. They were spiked directly to timber sleepers which had a semi-regular profile, and ballasted with stones, whose size varied from one to six inches in length. Construction materials which were shipped from Britain included the rails and cables for the telegraph lines connecting the new stations. Tenders for the civil engineering works were let out to local contractors, which accounts for the fact that while almost all stations on the system are built to the same general pattern, almost every one has some feature that sets it apart from its neighbour. The British influence did not extend as far as the railway's architecture, and station buildings have been likened to the style commonly found in France. The larger ones certainly tend to follow continental practice with the railway offices, passenger and parcel facilities downstairs, while the Stationmaster's living quarters occupy the upper floors.

Preparations for opening the new line were almost complete in 1874 when the rolling stock arrived aboard a fleet of ships including one Spanish and seven British steamers. At the time this was the largest collection of British merchant shipping ever seen in Palma. The three steam locomotives, six passenger carriages and twenty five goods vehicles were soon unloaded and transferred to the terminus at Palma. Majorca was at last about to enter the railway age.

Windmills were once a common sight in Majorca, both for grinding corn as well as raising underground water to the surface for irrigation.   (Collection - K. Taylorson)

Palma harbour in the days of sail.   (Collection - K. Taylorson)

Nasmyth Wilson photograph of an early 4-4-0 locomotive in its original form.   (Author's collection)

Chapter 2.
A History Of The Majorca Railway

The Railway Opens

The date set for the opening of the line was the 24th February 1875, and following a period of stormy weather the great day dawned bright and sunny. Outside the railway station at Palma two triumphal arches had been set up near the ruins of the old town walls at the Puerta Pintada (The Painted Gate); one had been provided by the Provincial Deputation, the other by the Ayunamiento (City Council) of Palma.In addition, at the station itself was another archway decorated with the coat of arms of each of the towns along the route, while the station buildings were bedecked with flags, flowers and branches of myrtle.

A large crowd had gathered and at nine o'clock the dignitaries arrived led by the Captain General of the Province who was followed by the Civil Governor, the Consular Corps, the Provincial Deputation and members of the Ayunamiento. After these came the railway's Directors and authorities and other distinguished guests. An open-air service was conducted on the platform before the V.I.Ps boarded the train which then set off for Inca. Crowds had turned out at all the stations but the train did not stop until it reached Inca, taking 64 minutes for the 29 kilometre journey.

Inca, like Palma, was in festive attire though here the streets were decorated in a more rustic style. Two local bands met the train and the whole procession moved through the garlanded streets to the town's main church where a Te Deum was sung. Following this the dignitaries returned to the station for a celebratory luncheon before making the return trip, this time taking the opportunity to inspect each of the stations along the line.

From the start the railway was a great success, no doubt helped by a policy of charging low fares:- 7 reals for a First Class ticket between Palma and Inca, 4.7 reals for Second Class. (A rough equivalent today would be 6 pence and 4 pence.) During its first month of operation the railway carried some 40,000 passengers, some days seeing as many as 6,000 travellers. Among them was the Spanish King, who visited the island in March 1876 and travelled to Inca by train on the 13th of the month. A special saloon coach was prepared for this journey which went without a hitch, setting the seal of royal approval on the railway.

Following the successful passenger opening the railway sought access for its goods trains to the harbour at Palma. As a direct route was barred by existing buildings, a street tramway through the city centre was opened in 1876 and soon helped to add to the company's profits.

Mergers and Expansion

These initial triumphs seem to have encouraged other potential railway schemes, for in 1876 the Compania de los Ferrocarriles del Centro y del Sureste (Central & South Eastern Railway Company) was formed. The new company produced a preliminary study for a route from Palma to Lluchmayor, leaving the existing railway at Pont D'Inca, and running via Sant Jordi. The following September a new study was undertaken for a line from Palma to Manacor via Coll d'En Rabassa, Son Veri and Lluchmayor. Not content with this the Central and South Eastern Company also announced their intention of building a line from Inca to Manacor via Sineu and Petra, with a branch line to serve La Puebla. While some of these goals were also the targets of the FC de Mallorca, their plans may not have been so far advanced as their rivals. However shortly afterwards the two railways merged as the Compania de los Ferrocarriles de Mallorca (Majorca Railways). Work on the extensions from Inca to Manacor and La Puebla started almost at once, while another more southerly route to Manacor via Felanitx was proposed and approved in the same year.

In preparation for the new extensions the company obtained 69,466 sleepers in 1877, costing between 88 cents and 1.25 pesetas each, with a total cost of 82,755 pesetas. Among the suppliers was Pedro Garau who was later to feature as Engineer for the construction of the FC de Soller (Soller Railway). In addition to sleepers the company also bought 750 telegraph poles and 15,000 fence posts. Earlier sleepers had been hand-sawn, but now

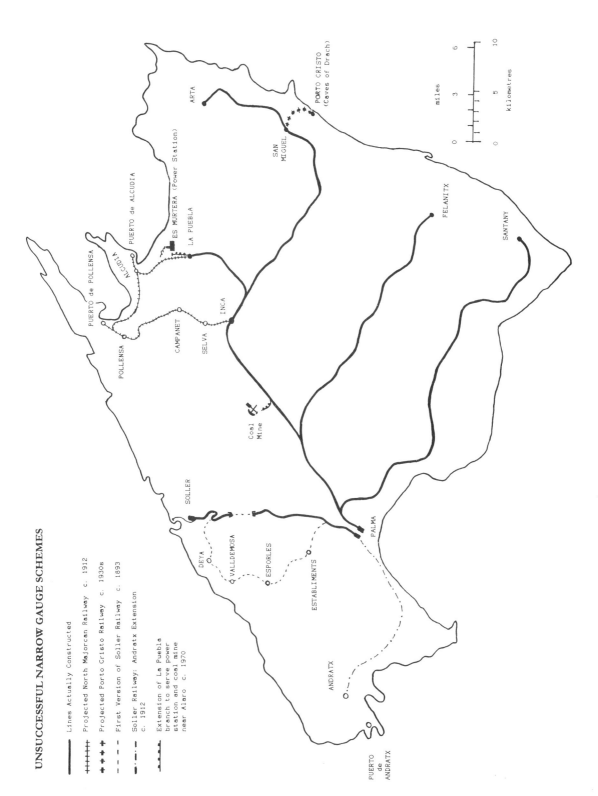

UNSUCCESSFUL NARROW GAUGE SCHEMES

Lines Actually Constructed

Projected North Majorcan Railway c. 1912

Projected Porto Cristo Railway c. 1930s

First Version of Soller Railway c. 1893

Soller Railway: Andratx Extension c. 1912

Extension of La Puebla branch to serve power station and coal mine near Alaro c. 1970

PUERTO de ANDRATX

ANDRATX

ESTABLIMENTS

ESPORLES

VALLDEMOSA

DEYA

SOLLER

PALMA

Coal Mine

POLLENSA

PUERTO de POLLENSA

CAMPANET

SELVA

INCA

ALCUDIA

PUERTO de ALCUDIA

ES MURTERA (Power Station)

LA PUEBLA

ARTA

SAN MIGUEL

PORTO CRISTO (Caves of Drach)

FELANITX

SANTANY

miles

kilometres

0   3   6

0   5   10

a steam-powered saw was imported from Britain and the work speeded up considerably, the saw being run day and night to complete the work. In addition a machine to inject all this timber with creosote also arrived from Britain on 21st September and had dealt with 32,000 sleepers, 400 telegraph poles and a small number of fence posts by the end of October.

Meanwhile trackbed grading had been proceeding across the centre of the island, though not without incident. Two contractors were involved in the work east of Inca, but one of them, Bartolomé Oliver, got into difficulties and had to be released from his contracted work between km 6.8 and km 10 which included an important bridge over the Torrente (river) Son Bordils. After a delay of a couple of months the contract was re-let to Manuel Lete, who was already responsible for the rest of the new main line extension and now finished the whole fourteen kilometres from Inca to Sineu, where a loading bank for goods traffic and a temporary station building (which survived in use until the 1920s) was erected by Pablo Togores. Palma workshops had constructed three turntables, one of which was given a home at Sineu when this was opened as a temporary terminus on 17th February 1878. Another may have gone to Empalme where traces of a former turntable can still be seen, while the third would have been needed at La Puebla.

The La Puebla branch was constructed by Nicolás Gelabert and Gabriel Llull who had completed the work in time for the inaugural service on 24th October 1878. This new branch was particularly important as it opened up the fertile northern farming region by providing direct access to the port of Palma. Hitherto goods traffic had been relatively unimportant between Palma and Inca, only averaging 30 tons per day in the early months of operation, but following the line's arrival at La Puebla freight tonnages started to increase dramatically, encouraged by the cheap rates of carriage. From a small village, La Puebla grew to become a busy town, due entirely to its situation as the railhead of the surrounding agricultural area.

The increased freight tonnages needed extra motive power in the shape of two 0-6-0 tank locomotives which were provided for goods and shunting duties, and a further four 4-4-0 tank engines which arrived in 1877 in good time to work the new services beyond Inca. Once again all these locomotives were obtained from Nasmyth Wilson. At the same time the Palma workshops were extended with a Carpenters' Shop and a Smithy, complete with two forges and machinery to re-profile the wheels of rolling stock. The new services required extra vehicles and during 1877 twenty wagons were added to the fleet, being built locally from parts imported from Britain at a total cost of 8,796 pesetas - a considerable saving over the cost of ready-built vehicles. Ever ready to pick up a bargain, the railway also acquired eight second-hand wagons for 1,200 pesetas. Neither were passengers neglected, as a further ten carriages and three brake-vans were purchased from British manufacturers. The railway's expansion continued when the section from Sineu to Manacor was opened in 1879. The turntable at Sineu was moved to the end of the new extension, and two additional 4-4-0 locomotives were obtained to work the extra traffic.

In 1881 the FC de Mallorca's monopoly of rail travel was broken when a line was built linking Consell station with the town of Alaró, a short distance away. The concession for this line was operated by the FC de Alaró (Alaró Railway). (For full details see Chapter 10).

Another innovation at about this time was the introduction of steam power for goods trains on the Palma Tramway. Hitherto mule-haulage had been employed, but in 1889 the Tramway acquired a four-coupled tank engine built by Nasmyth Wilson, works number 389. Unusually, perhaps, this locomotive does not seem to have been a true tramway type as the maker's photograph shows it devoid of the customary skirts provided to cover the wheels. When the locomotive used the harbour tramway a youth ringing a bell was sent ahead of the train to warn passers-by of its approach.

On the FC de Mallorca traffic continued to increase, and within a few years it began to outstrip the haulage capacity of the existing locomotive fleet. The railway company returned to Nasmyth's whose answer was to supply an enlarged version of the 4-4-0 type with an extra set of driving wheels and larger cylinders. Two of these 4-6-0s arrived in 1887 followed by another pair in 1891. Meanwhile in the same year, the Tramway appears to have acquired four steam trams, built by the Brush Electrical Engineering Company to an older

No. 5, one of the 0-6-0 shunting locomotives, seen at Palma on 2nd October 1957.   (L.G. Marshall)

COLL with two loaded coal wagons and brake van on the harbour branch at Palma in 1957.   (D. Trevor Rowe)

Falcon design. Little is known about them however, apart from their works numbers (198 - 201). Running numbers 2 - 5 were apparently allocated.

The railway's next major extension was the construction of the 43 kilometre branch to Felanitx which opened on 7th October 1897. Originally the Felanitx line was to have followed a slightly different course and was to have been extended to reach Manacor. A study of the proposed route had commenced in 1881 but following representations from several of the shareholders, who objected to the high cost of the project at a time when the island's economy was suffering a recession, the scheme was dropped. For the new line Nasmyth Wilson supplied yet another pair of 4-4-0 locomotives, though despite the increased traffic their cylinder capacity remained the same as the earlier members of their class.

For a while no new lines were added, perhaps to allow a few years of dividend payments to be made to the shareholders. Then in the early years of the new century more engines were added to the stock books. These were built by Palma Works, one in 1902 the other in the following year, and once again they were of the 4-4-0 type although this time larger cylinders were provided. They were also given extended main frames to carry longer tanks, and had larger diameter boilers. All the fabrication on these engines was carried out locally, only the wheels being imported. The two locomotives were characterised by their flared-topped chimneys, the Nasmyth engines carrying plain stove-pipe funnels. Following the successful introduction of these engines, Palma workshops undertook a programme of major conversion work on four of the older locomotives in 1911. Once again the size of the cylinders was increased to provide more power. New names and running numbers were allocated, the original names falling into disuse. The same year also saw what turned out to be the last new engines arrive from Nasmyth Wilson - yet another pair of 4-4-0 tanks. By this time the original 90 degree roundhouse at Palma was becoming inadequate to house the growing locomotive stud, and in 1913 it was extended to a full 180 degree layout.

Following the opening of the Felanitx branch, other Majorcan towns saw the advantages of having a railway connection with the rest of the island. As early as 1908 the citizens of Lluchmayor petitioned the island's Governor for a rail link, which could be built under the provisions of the newly passed Law of Secondary and Strategic Railways. It was envisaged that the line would serve Lluchmayor and continue by way of Campos to Santany. In December 1908 the Ministry formally invited the submission of plans for the line, but none had been presented by the closing date for submissions on July 20th 1910. Finally in 1913 a scheme drawn up by the railway's Engineer, Eusebio Estado, was submitted for approval. To raise sufficient capital for the line the Company offered four thousand shares worth 500 pesetas each. By 5th May this amount had been oversubscribed and 2.7 million pesetas had been offered. Despite this, some difficulties remained - the summer of 1913 saw local disputes among the citizens of Lluchmayor over the site of their proposed station, some maintaining that the chosen site was too small. Work on the track-bed started in 1914 but proceeded slowly to the fury of those who had subscribed for shares and felt that they were being cheated. Part of the delay was due to the fact that the route demanded some heavy engineering works, with a high bridge and two viaducts to be built near Arenal. Heavy rains during the winter of 1914-15 also delayed matters, but more importantly the outbreak of war in 1914 had cut the railway's connections with the British firms that had previously supplied rails and rolling stock, and new suppliers had to be found on the Spanish mainland. Eventually three 2-6-0 tank locomotives were obtained from La Maquinista Terrestre y Marítima of Barcelona. It had been hoped to begin services on the new branch in 1915, but in the end the line opened in three sections:- the 30 kms from Palma to Lluchmayor on 6th October 1916; the next 16 kms from Lluchmayor to Campos on 28th January 1917, with the final 17.5 kms to Santany entering service on 21st July of the same year.

At about this time the FC de Mallorca obtained its two smallest locomotives. The Palma Tramways had recently been electrified as a separate undertaking, and in 1917 the railway took over the Tramway's small Nasmyth locomotive, one of the Falcons having already found its way to the neighbouring Soller Railway, while the others seem to have been already laid aside as no further trace of them can be found. Soon after, in 1921, another 0-4-0 was acquired. This was a well tank built in Madrid by Orenstein & Koppel which was mainly used for working goods trains through the streets to the harbour together with general shunting duties at Palma.

MAJORCA RAILWAYS AND TRAMWAYS - AS BUILT

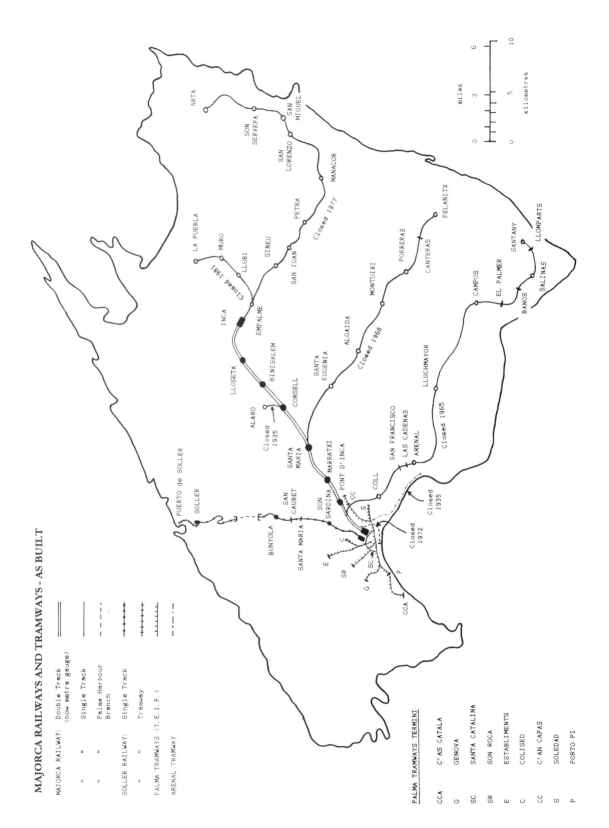

MAJORCA RAILWAY: Double Track (now metre gauge)

" " Single Track

" " Palma Harbour Branch

SOLLER RAILWAY: Single Track

" " Tramway

PALMA TRAMWAYS (T.E.I.P.)

ARENAL TRAMWAY

PALMA TRAMWAYS TERMINI

CCA   C'AS CATALA

G   GENOVA

SC   SANTA CATALINA

SR   SON ROCA

E   ESTABLIMENTS

C   COLISEO

CC   C'AN CAPAS

S   SOLEDAD

P   PORTO PI

The Railway's Heyday

The railway entered the 1920's with the traffic potential still increasing, bolstered no doubt by the resumption of world trade after the cessation of hostilities. Once again plans were made to expand the company's empire with extensions from Manacor to Arta and Porto Cristo, and from La Puebla to Alcudia and Pollensa. By the summer of 1921 the line had reached Arta and this proved to be the last addition to passenger mileage, as the other extensions never materialised. To work the Arta services the company obtained six powerful 2-6-0 tank engines from Krupp in 1926.

In complete contrast, the company also acquired another vehicle in 1926 that was an early indication of the future, and foreshadowed the ultimate end of steam power. In its early form the four-wheeled 40hp petrol driven railcar built by Berliet cannot have seemed much of a threat, with its relatively small seating capacity and limited haulage powers. However it proved its worth on the more lightly patronised lines, and in 1930 three De Dion railcars were added to the fleet, becoming the mainstay of the services to Santany and Felanitx.

Soon afterwards the company added yet more motive power to its books with the purchase of some even larger tank locomotives, this time from Babcock and Wilcox of Bilbao. These 2-6-2Ts went into service in 1930 and had the capability of running between Palma and Manacor without a water stop, unlike the earlier engines that had to top up their tanks at Inca and Manacor in order to reach Arta. Once again the new locomotive purchases called for more shed space at Palma, where a second roundhouse was completed in 1930. To go with the new motive power the company obtained fourteen bogie carriages from Carde y Escoriaza.

With the general increase in traffic and the opening of the Arta extension, the single line out of Palma reached the limits of its capacity. It had become the custom to combine trains to La Puebla and Arta as far as Inca, double heading them to get over this section's worst gradients between Pont D'Inca and Consell. However when even this expedient was no longer enough, the decision was taken to double the main line as far as Inca. The new track was laid with heavier rails weighing 30kgs/metre and the new section was completed in January 1931. At the same time the task of working goods trains through the streets of Palma was abandoned when a new tunnel was opened linking the port with the goods yard at the railway terminus. These services were subsequently worked by the 4-4-0 tanks. The Nasmyth 0-4-0T seems to have faded away at an unrecorded date, but the Orenstein & Koppel lingered on for another thirty years or so in a semi-derelict state.

During the early 1930's the fortunes of the company reached their peak, but after the Civil War a slow decline set in. Road competition began to be a serious factor and the railway could no longer claim a virtual monopoly on the movement of goods traffic. Another setback came in 1936 when the Berliet railcar caught fire and was almost completely destroyed. Although the railcar had proved useful at first, its engine was in a very poor state by this time.

The outbreak of the Second World War again caused a locomotive famine, and this time the FC de Mallorca turned to its neighbour the FC de Soller which had been electrified some years previously and so had five surplus steam locomotives laid up at Palma. One was the Falcon-built 0-4-0 tram locomotive formerly used by the Palma Tramways, while the others were 2-6-0 tanks built by La Maquinista, similar to those already operating on the FC de Mallorca. All five were purchased although the Falcon and one of the larger engines were almost immediately condemned and scrapped.

By the end of the war the railway was in a poor condition, suffering from years during which maintenance had been run down or deliberately neglected. Casualties at this time were the first two Nasmyth 4-4-0 engines, MAJORCA and PALMA which were laid up in 1945 and 1948 respectively. The Orenstein & Koppel appears to have been taken off the active list at about the same time. As the older locomotives were withdrawn they were cannibalised for parts to keep the rest of the fleet running. The railway struggled on, and despite a reputation for being dirty and slow, still managed to move considerable amounts of passengers and freight. By now separate passenger workings had been suspended and all trains were being run "mixed". The resulting poor timekeeping helped to drive yet more potential passengers away, though the poor quality of the locomotive coal, resulting in bad steaming and slower running also contributed to the decline. By the start of the

1950's the company could continue no longer and even had to suspend all services to Arta, Santany and Felanitx for a week in early 1951. Following prolonged negotiations, the Ministry of Works took over the lines belonging to the FC de Mallorca from 1st August 1951. The new management was known as Explotación de Ferrocarriles por el Estado, or E.F.E.

The Nationalisation Era

The new regime immediately introduced a policy of cost cutting and an early decision was to reduce services to two trains per day on each line to enable the viable members of the locomotive stud to undergo necessary overhauls and to weed out the life-expired machines. Of the entire fleet only two locomotives, numbers 9 and 55 were in good condition, while a further eight were in a reasonable state (four 4-4-0s, 2 Krupps and 2 Babcocks). All the rest were in poor condition while four of the 4-4-0s were past further use, including number 3 which was scrapped in 1959. With such a large programme of repairs Palma works took on nine locomotives between 1952 and 1955, while the rest were repaired by other firms including MTM, Babcock & Wilcox, Sucecoral S.A. and Astiller of Palma. The two Nasmyth 0-6-0 locomotives were found to be fit enough to remain in service for shunting duties, which they took over from the Orenstein & Koppel locomotive. When they were finally withdrawn they had then been in continuous use for all but two years of the railway's history.

With the beginnings of the Majorcan tourist boom one of the weaknesses of the local rail system became apparent: almost nowhere, with the exception of Arenal, did it serve the beaches that were to be so important to the island's expanding economy. Added to this, the railway did not present a very attractive aspect being old, dirty, uncomfortable and slow, although an attempt to improve matters had been made on the Santany branch when some of the original four-wheeled coaches were painted white and blue to act as trailers for the elderly De Dion railcars between Palma and Arenal.

A fresh policy was obviously needed, as well as considerable capital expenditure, and various Ministry studies were undertaken to look at different modernisation methods. Electrification was impossible to justify as traffic levels varied so much between the different branch lines, and such a scheme would depend on total conversion to allow stock to be used efficiently. However it was obvious that the days of steam power were numbered, and in 1956 a policy of complete dieselisation was implemented with the introduction of four bogie railcars built by Esslingen in Germany. Six matching trailers were also supplied. Then in 1959 four Krupp-designed diesel-hydraulic B-B locomotives were obtained, which were built under license in Bilbao. These were needed to maintain the mixed train services, to Arta and La Puebla. The new policy gathered momentum when two more railcars and four more trailers came into service. They were outwardly identical to the 1956 batch, but had been built by Euskalduna. The new diesels together with the earlier railcars were now able to handle all the passenger services and steam withdrawals speeded up.

The introduction of the diesels resulted in the reinstatement of some services. Except for the Felanitx branch, which only saw two daily railcars and the occasional goods train, all the other lines were soon back to three daily services, some of them running as mixed trains - these workings perhaps providing the final steam duties. Santany's three trains were all railcars however. As a whole the railway was still operating as a "general carrier", and freight tonnage for 1960 totalled 84,100 tons, carried in 493 wagons. The passenger fleet comprised 56 carriages, ranging from the earliest Brown Marshall vehicles up to the bogie coaches of the 1930s, plus the railcars. By 1963 the timetable showed all scheduled services being run by railcars, mixed trains having disappeared and the goods traffic that remained being run separately. Steam power was finally withdrawn from the FC de Mallorca on 12th December 1964.

Another Change Of Management

In 1965 control of the Majorca Railway (together with other nationalised narrow gauge lines on the Spanish mainland) were transferred from E.F.E. to a new organisation:- FEVE (Ferrocarriles Españoles de Vía Estrecha, or Spanish Narrow Gauge Railways.)

Despite the economies effected by the introduction of the railcar fleet, the railway system continued a slow contraction although outside factors also played a part. By the mid 1960s the increasing demands of tourism called for the extension of Palma airport. Part of the Santany branch stood in the way of this progress

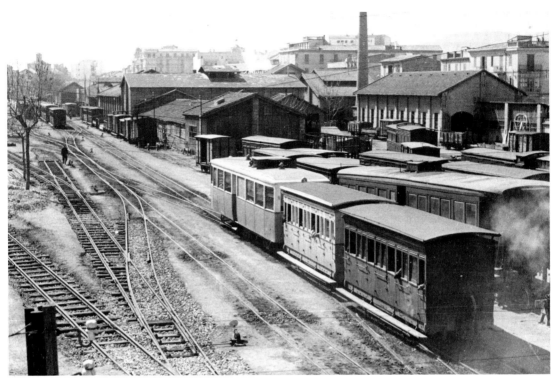

Nearing journey's end at Palma, a De Dion railcar towing two coaches passes the workshops on 17th March 1958. Note the lines leading into the goods yard are being relaid.   (J. Wiseman)

Railcar A4 towing a Correo/2nd class coach leaves Palma for Santany on 2nd October 1957.   (L.G. Marshall)

and so the line was closed on 4th March 1965, though it is ironic that the growth of tourism should have swept away the one branch that might have been of use to the increasing numbers of visitors.

By this time the harbour line was all but derelict, the recorded tonnage in 1965 being the equivalent of one wagon load. Elsewhere however things seemed more hopeful, at least for passenger services. Three trains a day had been restored on the other lines and in addition there were now four new "short" services on the main line, three terminating at Inca, the other at Manacor. The optimism of these new services was slightly tarnished on 31st December 1967 when the Felanitx branch together with the Palma harbour line were officially closed. At the same time all freight carriage ceased, goods traffic receipts having been in decline since nationalisation. The cessation of goods services meant that the diesel locomotives were now something of a luxury, and eventually all were returned to the mainland.

Even after the take-over by FEVE the future of the railway was uncertain. As the line was run from Madrid it tended to suffer from the resulting bureaucracy, with decisions having to be ratified at State level rather than locally; this tended to result in stagnation. At the end of the 1960s the service comprised 11 daily trips between Palma and Inca (plus one extra on Sundays). Four of these workings continued to Arta and another four to La Puebla. By 1972 timings had been improved and the number of services to and from Inca had increased to 16, though after 26th October 1974 one of these was dropped again. However, little maintenance was being done and the threat of closure was never far away from the section beyond Manacor where the number of daily services to Arta was cut from four to three railcars per day from 1st December 1974.

By the early 1970s the railway had a deficit of 38 million pesetas. Passenger figures showed 1,000,200 journeys of which 950,000 were made between Palma and Inca. In the circumstances FEVE may not have felt much like celebrating the Centenary of the line in early 1975. However the City Council of Palma and the local Tourist Board had other ideas. At first they hoped to run a steam service, but it was pointed out that all the locomotives had been scrapped some years previously. In the event a railcar and two trailers ran the Centenary service, which was also marked by the unveiling of a plaque at Palma station. The occasion was attended by the President of FEVE, and in the speeches grandiose plans were outlined, including electrification of the system and the re-opening of the old tunnel to the harbour. A station would be built under the Plaza España with a new waterfront terminus at the Parque del Mar, near the Cathedral. All this would render the present terminus redundant, and the site would be sold to help defray the costs of the scheme. However, following the upheavals of the celebrations the railway returned to more mundane operations, while official pronouncements as to the future of the line resumed their customary vagueness for a while.

The continuing size of the operating deficit meant that new cuts were sought in the following years, and eventually the economics of running the Arta services caught up with the line. Following a derailment at Petra which needed a crane to rectify the damage, the section between Empalme and Arta was closed "provisionally" on 20th June 1977, but rather than commit heavy re-investment into track renewals it was obvious that a FEVE-operated bus service provided a more economic answer, and the closure became permanent.

The gradual run-down of services caused a glut of redundant rolling stock at Palma, where desultory attempts were made to scrap them. Finally in September 1978, the company decided to burn the survivors, and the resulting scrap metal was sold off at 7 pesetas per kilo. Two of the bogie carriages were saved, one being converted into a house, the other preserved intact together with a handful of dropside open wagons, a few flat trucks and one brake van which were retained for use on ballast trains.

Despite the large numbers of tourists visiting Majorca by this time, no effort seems to have been made to encourage them to use the FEVE services. Local information at the stations could be unreliable and likely to be countermanded by chalked announcements on a blackboard, while the published timetables had copious footnotes in Spanish, all of which was liable to deter the casual traveller. Nevertheless limited numbers of tourists were using the railway, in contrast to the FC de Soller which was actively promoting its tourist potential. Meanwhile the FEVE line was left to the local inhabitants though as some of the competing bus services were faster than the trains this was perhaps a dangerous policy to pursue.

The 1980s - Worsening Problems and Some Solutions

In 1980 the Spanish Government commissioned a report on Balearic transport, and the sections dealing with Majorca's two railways made bleak reading. On the FEVE line the section between Palma and Inca was in a reasonable state, but beyond here the line to La Puebla was in a bad condition, the section from Inca to Empalme needing complete replacement. The FEVE workshops' equipment was largely obsolete, and only light repairs were possible while major work was being contracted out at a cost of 4 to 8 million pesetas a year. As a result the railcar fleet, despite being within its recommended life expectancy of 25-30 years, had suffered from insufficient maintenance and the continual pounding received from the indifferent permanent way, and a large investment would be needed to rectify matters. The report noted that much of the site of the Palma terminus was under-used, as was the old railway tunnel to the port. Various station buildings were suffering from damp, and required repairs.

A major concern was public safety at the 112 level crossings on the Palma - La Puebla line. Of these only 15 were provided with barriers. (The average distance between level crossings was 2.4 kilometres.) Incidents between trains and road transport were not uncommon, and there had been a fatal accident in the outskirts of Palma recently. It was also noted that the line was run with the trains' movements merely being advised locally from station to station by telephone - a method that lacked a certain sophistication by 1980. In addition the crossing keepers were not included on the telephone circuit and had to rely on their knowledge of the timetable and the warning whistles of approaching trains. In its favour it has to be said that this system had catered in the past for a higher traffic density than the present two services an hour. The report found that the infrequency of services and their general unreliability had led to a falling passenger demand over the years, which had not been offset by the railway's policy of charging lower passenger fares per kilometre that the competing bus services. In fact the practise had merely helped to speed the slide into deficit.

In conclusion the report made certain suggestions:-

1. Provide more stations in the Palma - Marratxi section, where the new outskirts of the capital were poorly served.

2. Introduce signalling and C.T.C., and improve the railway's telephone system.

3. Improve the state of the permanent way and provide extra passing loops.

4. Provide automatic level crossing barriers to comply with current legislation.

5. Modernise the workshops, possibly on a new site.

6. Modernise the rolling stock. (A two-year plan already existed to spend 16 million pesetas on rebuilding two of the railcars with a further 6 million going towards upgrading four of the trailers.)

7. Close the section from Inca to La Puebla.

8. Reduce staffing levels in three areas:- by the provision of automatic level crossings, by turning all the intermediate stations into unstaffed halts, and by issuing tickets on the trains.

9. Introduce a gradual fare increase to a level where costs could be covered, and abolish the concessionary rates currently offered.

10. Undertake further studies to see whether better use of the Palma terminus could be achieved. This could involve making a new connection with the FC de Soller beyond the station throat and bringing both lines into a shared terminus, thus eliminating several urban level crossings on the Soller line.

11. Undertake a study of the benefits of a Metro, using the old goods tunnel (in effect a resurrection of the Centenary scheme.)

12. Undertake a study of the possible benefits of re-introducing a passenger and goods service (coal traffic only) between Palma, Inca and Alcudia.

While the report gave the gauge of the island's railways as 3 feet it did not recommend a conversion to metre gauge. However such a change had several potential benefits including the possibility of greater speeds and consequently better utilisation of line capacity. Shorter journey times could help to woo traffic back from road transport, while the ability to transfer metre gauge rolling stock from other FEVE lines on the mainland could help combat the problems posed by a rapidly ageing railcar fleet.

As regards goods services GESA, the local power company, were planning to build a power station at Es Murtera, between La Puebla and Alcudia, and a scheme was drawn up to supply coal by rail from the mines near Consell via a 7.5 kilometre extension of the line beyond La Puebla and a partial re-opening of the old Alaró branch. It was envisaged that 1,000,000 tonnes of coal a year could be carried, although the track on the coal carrying portion of the line would have to be upgraded from 30 to 40kg/metre rail. However other experts questioned whether the mines had sufficient reserves to meet this demand. The possibility of extending the line to Es Murtera temporarily revived the earlier plans to include Alcudia and Pollensa on the railway map. The increased speeds possible with new metre gauge track would reduce the journey to La Puebla from one and a quarter hours to forty-five minutes, thus the extra distance might be achieved within the original timetable slot. The existing number of railcars would allow eighteen workings between Palma and Alcudia and fourteen services to Inca were planned. However, ultimately the decision was taken not to proceed with the extension.

By 1981 the balance sheet was still in the red, to the tune of 185.6 million pesetas. Nevertheless the closures of 1977 had helped to bring the figures down from their previous annual totals; the sum spent on stations being reduced by 5.6 million pesetas while the savings on fixed installations and plant totalled 4.3 million pesetas. It appears that a combination of cuts and savings were also practised in the railway's workshops where spending fell by 6.3 million pesetas over the same period. However, other costs rose:- Train Operation by almost 6 million pesetas and General Costs by nearly 4 million, though Road Services achieved a small saving. In 1981 passengers carried by rail numbered 931,159 up from 887,218 the previous year, and earning just over 36.8 million pesetas, to which road transport added a further 5 million pesetas.

Despite the deficit the metre gauge conversion was implemented between Palma and Inca, although the section onward to La Puebla was closed from 31st March 1981. The right hand running line out of Palma was altered first, trains in 1981 using the old 3ft gauge track alongside for bi-directional travel. This entailed passenger trains running via the workshop line at Palma as the rest of the station approach had been lifted to

Railcar and trailer leaving Palma bound for Inca in 1981. The workshop loop provides the only access to the main line as the station approach has been lifted for metre gauge track-laying.   (Author)

install the new metre gauge tracks. The conversion was started from both ends of the line and was completed by 1983. At the same time as the gauge conversion, colour light signalling was also installed, as well as automatic half-barriers at major level crossings.

In the late 1980s plans were laid to open a new station to serve a proposed megastore just outside Palma. However a failure of investment ultimately caused the collapse of the project; nevertheless the suburbs of Palma are shortly going to benefit from the introduction of three new halts, one at kilometre 3.7 named Virgen del Lluch. The de-staffing of the original stations has brought with it problems of vandalism, and to counteract this concessions for cantinas (cafes) are to be granted in all stations, providing a measure of protection. Eventually the cantinas will also be responsible for issuing railway tickets and looking after the station car parks.

By the end of the 1980s a new policy was in force for the FEVE lines, which were gradually handed back to be run by the local autonomous regions, though this has yet to happen in Majorca where negotiations regarding the underwriting of costs are yet to be completed. Another possibility currently complicating negotiations is a possible merger between FEVE and RENFE, the nationalised broad gauge railway system. However, it does seem that the transfer is likely to take place by 1995.

The late 1980s were a difficult time for major investment and while Spain's membership of the European Community might have been thought to be a way to obtaining money for re-development of the FEVE system, the Balearic Islands are low on the E.C. priority list for grants. Meanwhile, following a serious fire at Palma which destroyed the carriage shed including several railcars and trailers, the surviving life-expired railcars have at last been replaced with a number of 2-car DMUs built by MAN which arrived in September 1991, having been transferred from FEVE's Santander-Orviedo line in Northern Spain. In addition 200 million pesetas is to be spent on major track renovations in the near future, while 1992 will see the development of the derelict goods yard area to provide car parking facilities and a new bus station. This work will almost certainly result in the demolition of the old goods shed.

The railway has continued to be the subject of study projects. One carried out at the end of the 1980s recommended rebuilding at least part of the old main line, which is currently closed, and the decision to proceed with this has been taken in principle. It is likely that 40-45 kg/metre rail will be used together with cut-down second hand sleepers from RENFE. Initially the renovation might result in services to Sineu being restored, and depending on the commercial outcome of this renewal it may prove worthwhile to re-open more of the old main line, with Manacor as an eventual goal.

New safety measures provided recently include automatic crossing barriers, like these at Santa Maria. (Author)

21

SALINAS exhibits the flared chimney typical of the 4-4-0Ts built by Palma workshops. (Brian Butt)

A comparison of sizes between a Nasmyth Wilson 4-4-0T and one of the Maquinista 2-6-0Ts. (J. Wiseman)

Chapter 3
FC de Mallorca Motive Power

The 4-4-0 Tanks.

In the early days the Majorca Railway patronised British firms for both rolling stock and motive power, the latter being supplied by Nasmyth Wilson of Patricroft, Leeds, who continued to do so until their connection with the island was severed by the First World War.

The first three locomotives to be supplied for the opening of the line had a 4-4-0 wheel arrangement. They had a rather short boiler and firebox, while the frames were raised above the front bogie to support the smokebox, with the cylinders bolted onto this upward extension at an inclined angle. The bogie wheels were of a solid pattern with raised spokes; above them the locomotive's frames extended forwards from below the smokebox to carry a wooden buffer beam and a cow-catcher. The original cabs were little more than a pair of shaped weatherboards supporting the roof. Names and numbers were allocated to this trio, which became MAJORCA, PALMA and INCA. They weighed a mere 15.8 tonnes.

In 1877 four similar Nasmyth locomotives were obtained, and these were named SINEU, LA PUEBLA, SANTA MARIA and BINISALEM. These machines had an increased wheelbase and enlarged cylinders. The next arrivals in 1881 were named MURO and PETRA, and had still larger cylinders reflecting the increasing traffic of the times. Another significant alteration that became standard from now on was the enlargement of the boiler while the firebox size was also increased. Finally in 1879 another pair of 4-4-0s named PORRERAS and MONTUIRI were brought into service. These locomotives were also the larger type and weighed 16.3 tonnes.

The twentieth century saw the first engines emerge from the workshops at Palma. Once again they weighed 16.3 tonnes and with a burst of patriotism, no doubt to celebrate the Spanish King's sixteenth birthday, they were named ALFONSO XIII (built 1902) and ESPAÑA (built 1903). (Later in Republican days ALFONSO was renamed SALINAS.) Both engines were once again back in the workshops in 1911 for a rebuild which resulted in their weight being increased another half a tonne. The same year also saw the locomotives obtained in 1877, as well as one of the 1881 batch, undergoing similar rebuilding which resulted in a weight of 16.8 tonnes. The original names were dropped, the set now being called COLL, SAN MIGUEL, SAN LORENZO, ARTA and SON SERVERA.

After 1911 the 4-4-0s remained an active part of the locomotive stud, though no doubt they were rostered on lighter duties with the advent of more powerful machines. For instance the original three locomotives were only allocated to work the slower trains to Santany and Felanitx, while on the Arta line they were confined to goods trains or the slow Mixed services. The first withdrawals seem to have come at the end of the Second World War when MAJORCA and PALMA were finally put aside and scrapped. Roughly ten years later INCA, MONTUIRI, SAN MIGUEL, SAN LORENZO and SON SERVERA were withdrawn. The remainder seem to have survived until the general withdrawal of steam power in the 1960s, although by the end only one is recorded as still being active. The honour of being the last-known working survivor seems to have gone to ARTA in 1957, though COLL was also recorded shunting the harbour branch in the same year, and SALINAS too is also known to have been on the active list shortly before this date.

The 0-6-0 Tanks.

Shortly after the line's original opening the need for more locomotives became apparent, resulting in the arrival of two 0-6-0s from Nasmyth Wilson in 1876. To give extra power the size of the cylinders was increased to 330mm by 457mm. These new locomotives weighed 16.2 tonnes and proved to be ideally suited to their function of shunting and goods haulage. They were allocated the names MANACOR and FELANITX and remained in service until the final steam withdrawals.

The 4-6-0 Tanks.

The extensions of the late 1880's and the increasing tonnage of trains began to demand a heavier class of locomotive. Nasmyth's answer was a 4-6-0 design that was virtually a larger version of the goods tanks with a

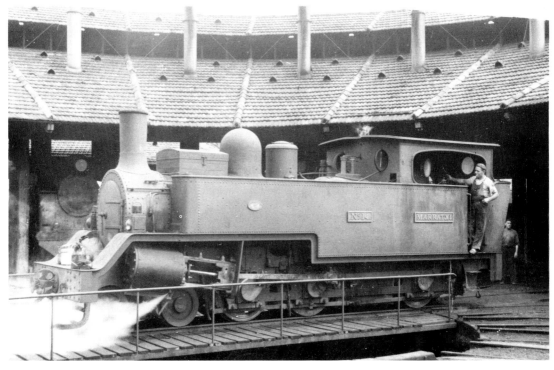

MARRATXI eases onto the turntable at Palma roundhouse.   (L.G. Marshall)

Krupp-built 2-6-0 No 30 at Palma.   (L.G. Marshall)

leading bogie and larger cylinders. The extra length was used to advantage as the tanks were extended and for the first time a continuous footplate was provided. The bogie wheels were unlike the earlier engines as they were of the disc variety pierced by six holes. At first the engines were given a very small coal bunker but operating on inferior coal brought about the alteration of this feature in later life to give a greater fuel capacity.

Two engines of this class, SAN JUAN and LLOSETA were put into service in 1887 with two more, MARRATXI and ALARO, being added in 1891. Finally in 1911 another pair named ALGAIDA and SANTA EUGENIA were obtained. As a class they lasted until the end of the steam era, being employed in later years on troop trains and freight workings. In 1957 four were still active, these being SAN JUAN, LLOSETA, MARRATXI and ALARO. ALGAIDA is also reported as being active during 1957 and pictorial evidence exists of her in steam at Palma in 1955. She appears to have been allocated to Felanitx from 1959 but by 1960 she was to be found there partially dismantled.

The Maquinista 2-6-0 Tanks.

With the opening of the Santany branch in 1917 yet more engines were needed, however as the war had cut the established links with Great Britain the company turned to La Maquinista Terrestre y Marítima of Barcelona who provided three locomotives similar to those built for the neighbouring FC de Soller. These new purchases were the largest engines owned by the FC de Mallorca, although they did not enjoy this distinction for long. As usual the new arrivals were given local names, becoming LLUCHMAYOR, CAMPOS and SANTANY. Later, when another World War caused a locomotive famine on the island the FC de Mallorca obtained their neighbour's remaining MTM engines which had been lying derelict at Palma station ever since the Soller line's electrification in 1929. One of them and the original contractor's locomotive were scrapped at once, but the three survivors put in another fifteen year's service, becoming numbers 7, 8 and 9. (For some reason the names that vanished in the 1911-era rebuilding programme were not re-used). All the Maquinista locomotives lasted well into the final days of steam, being often employed on the La Puebla services in the late 1950's, though numbers 7,8 and 9 were reportedly withdrawn by 1960. No.19 LLUCHMAYOR seems to have been a particular favourite working on a variety of services. By June 1960 she was stored at Palma, while No. 21 SANTANY was still active.

The German 2-6-0 Tanks.

To cope with the gradients of the Arta section, together with its long stretches between water supplies, the company again felt the need for some more powerful locomotives; thus in 1926 they purchased six engines with a 2-6-0 wheel arrangement from Krupp of Essen. These newcomers were numbered   30 to 35 and appeared towards the end of August, the honour of being the first in service falling to number 34 on the 21st of the month. The other engines followed at roughly three day intervals, the final pair, 31 and 35 appearing on August 30th. The new class were superheated and had slightly larger driving wheels and cylinders than the MTM locomotives. As a class they brought a belated twentieth century look to the motive power department with an electric headlamp which also displayed the running number on an illuminated panel on each side. Another innovation was the provision of a conventional hook and screw-up coupling set below the narrow gauge "chopper".

The 2-6-2 Tanks.

The final development of steam power on the Majorcan railway system took the form of a set of six 2-6-2 tank engines numbered 50-55, built by Babcock & Wilcox of Bilbao in 1930. Four of these went into service during the last three months of that year, though possibly there were teething troubles as the final two emerged after slight modification the following year, No 52 on 28th February and No 55 on 6th March. The new engines which were also superheated, displayed several new features including feed water heaters, and were capable of running from Palma to Manacor without a water stop. Some of the class were fitted with vacuum hoses on the front buffer beam, so this could have been part of the modifications that delayed the introduction of the last two members of this type. This equipment appears only in pictures of number 55 as running in 1953, and had been removed by 1957.

The final development of Majorcan steam power - Babcock & Wilcox No 53 at Manacor on 13th August 1962.

(J.K. Williams)

Maker's photograph of Nasmyth-built 0-4-0 showing the original chimney, later changed to a stove pipe type, and couplings for tramway use.

(Author's collection)

A rare view of the Orenstein & Koppel locomotive seen here at Palma shed in 1958.

(J. Wiseman)

The 0-4-0 Tanks.

The FC de Mallorca owned two small locomotives which were primarily used to haul goods trains through the streets to the docks before the harbour tunnel was built. The older locomotive, built in 1889, was another from Nasmyth Wilson - an 0-4-0T weighing 12.5 tonnes. Originally it had been supplied to the Palma Tramways who passed it on to the railway company in 1917. The maker's photograph shows that a conventional hook coupling and traditional buffing gear was fitted at first, together with a tall capped chimney. Later Palma Works fitted a stovepipe chimney as well as chopper couplings and side chains. It became number 6 on the company's books and was nicknamed "LA INGLESITA" (Little English Girl). Latterly derelict, number 6 does not seem to have been broken up until about 1955.

The other four-coupled locomotive was an Orenstein and Koppel design built under license in Madrid in 1921, and which became number 7 on the railway company's books. This number was re-allocated in 1944 and the O & K lingered on un-numbered until about 1960, by which time its shunting duties had been taken over by the two 0-6-0Ts.

FC de Mallorca steam engine livery was green, perhaps originally lined out round the edges of the tanks with a thick black band; this style is certainly in evidence on one of the 0-6-0 shunters as late as 1957, although the other Nasmyth engines show no hint of any lining. Eye-witnesses in later years speak of the locomotives being an indeterminate colour combining a lack of fresh paintwork with a patina of coal dust. It is probable that only the Nasmyth engines were painted green, and that the Spanish and German locomotives were black.

The Early Railcars.

During the 1920s the FC de Mallorca turned to internal combustion as a way of saving money on lightly patronised services. The first railcar was built by Berliet in March 1926 (works number 9); on arrival in Majorca it was given the number A-1. The four-wheeled vehicle had a doorway towards the rear of the body on each side, and thirty seated passengers could be carried. Although no luggage space was provided the 40hp engine was capable of hauling a couple of the smaller carriages when necessary, so this was not an insuperable problem. The drive was by mechanical transmission to one axle, however the vehicle was dogged by a succession of mechanical breakdowns in the early days, no doubt due to the operating staff's lack of experience with internal combustion engines. A-1 does not seem to have been popular with the crews who thought its engine was "lousy", and it may already have been out of use in 1935 when it caught fire at Inca. After this the remains were stored at Manacor for many years. Unlike the later railcars A-1 was a single ended vehicle with a radiator at the front of the body, but this would have been no particular operating disadvantage given the number of turntables on the system.

The advantages of railcar use led to another three vehicles being brought into service in the summer of 1931. These had bodies constructed by Werkspoor NV of Amsterdam, while their running gear and the 85hp diesel engines, whose 4 cylinders measured 125 by 150mm, were supplied by the Société des Automobiles De Dion-Bouton of Puteux, France. Their top speed was 55km/hr. Like A-1 they were four-wheeled vehicles with a long rigid wheelbase which must have made them rough riders. The seating capacity was 40 passengers, and a toilet compartment was provided. The radiators were mounted centrally on the roof with large air scoops facing in either direction. Livery at first was light blue below the waist, with white above, the two colours being separated by a narrow band of scarlet beading. The running number was displayed over the end doors. As well as passenger duties they were also useful on light p.w. tasks when their ability to carry a work crew and haul a wagon or two was used to full advantage.

During the 1950s in an effort to present a smarter image to any potential tourist traffic some of the old four-wheeled compartment coaches were painted to match the railcars. These were used on the Arenal/Santany services, whereas the normal trailer on the Felanitx branch at this time was an old Postal/2nd class composite carriage which had retained its original brown livery. After 1951 under State ownership the livery of the original railcars changed to dark green below the waist and very pale grey-green above. There was a horizontal band of this paler colour just below the top of the green panel.

Esslingen-built railcar in all-blue livery at Palma in 1977.   (K. Taylorson)

One of the 2-car dmu sets which have been transferred to Majorca to replace the older railcars. Palma, January 1992.
(Author)

In April 1952 A-3 caught fire and was burnt out, resulting in a complete rebuild. This may be the reason why the original motors were replaced with Berliet engines between 1954 and 1956. The two survivors (numbers A-2 and A-3) were last recorded at Palma in August 1979 though by then they may not have been in daily use.

The Bogie Railcars.

In the interests of standardisation E.F.E. undertook a wholesale programme of dieselisation on all its lines during the late 1950s. Twenty five bogie railcars were obtained from Ferrostaal, some apparently coming from the Esslingen factory while others were manufactured under license by Euskalduna of Bilbao. These were given the running numbers 2001 - 2006 and 2011 - 2029, although not all of these appeared in Majorca.

The original Majorcan allocation were railcars 2001 to 2004 which arrived in 1956. Apparently the original order was for five vehicles but the first one to be delivered was metre gauge, as the news of the Majorca Railway's odd gauge had seemingly failed to reach the factory. Urgent telegrams ensured that the following deliveries were the correct gauge. The Majorcan batch of railcars had been built at Esslingen (works numbers 23782/56 - 23785/56.) Each was capable of carrying a total of 95 passengers (54 seated, 41 standing) and the principle dimensions were as follows:- Overall length 15 metres, Overall width 2.45 metres, height (above rail) 3.4 metres. Bogie centres were 10 metres apart and the bogie wheelbase was 1.6 metres. The driving controls included foot pedals for the throttle and whistle, with a manually operated gear lever and brake handle. These new units had Bussing motors capable of speeds up to 75 km/hr, which had an immediately beneficial effect on the timetable.

Another pair of railcars, numbers 2005 and 2006, arrived in 1958 and eventually the total rose to nine vehicles, although by 1979 the number had been reduced to six units, three having suffered fires. The railcars then in service were 2002, 2004 - 2006, 2019 and 2027. The problem of overheating was finally cured by replacing the original 150 hp Bussing motors with 250 hp Pegaso engines.

To go with the new bogie railcars several matching trailers were provided. These can be distinguished by having no headlamp above the central door in the car ends, and by being numbered in the 5000 series. Originally they all had a toilet and a mail section, but 5001 and 5003-4 were rebuilt soon after their arrival to give a total passenger accommodation of 100. For a time 5002 retained its a postal compartment at one end, which was designated by the exterior end panels below window level being painted yellow, but it was also rebuilt to match the others at the end of the 1980s. Another trailer (5018) is of a different design as it has no luggage compartment, making it about 2.5 metres shorter than the others.

Over the years the Majorcan bogie railcars have carried four different liveries. At first they were painted two-tone green with ESTADO in metal letters on the side panels. This paint scheme was recorded on 2001 in 1960, and on 2004 and 2019 as late as 1974. However by the latter date most of the fleet had been repainted as the change of control of the line from E.F.E. to FEVE resulted in a second livery of medium light blue with thick and thin horizontal stripes below window level and another thick stripe above. The roof was silver. This scheme was certainly carried by 2004, 2005 and 2019 during the 1970s, and also by trailers 5003, 5005 and 5018.

A new version of the FEVE livery was introduced around 1980. Midnight blue lower bodywork was set off by "spilt milk" above the waist. The FEVE logo of a double-track crossover within a circle and all lettering and numbers were white. The latest FEVE livery, outshopped from 1989, is white bodywork with a simple style of lettering. Vehicle roofs are painted yellow. Once again there has been an overlap of liveries, as a visit in December 1991 turned up one railcar still in blue and cream, while several other vehicles were still in the earlier all blue colour scheme - although these appeared to be derelict. A further four or five units had suffered fires, rendering identification impossible.

Although the second generation railcars were arranged to be coupled in multiple units when necessary, the trailers have no driving controls. It is thus necessary for the railcars to run round their trailers after each journey.

B-B diesel locomotive No 1102 leaving Palma for Santany on 10th June 1960.   (Mike Swift)

Diesel shunter and ballast train - Palma yard 1981.   (Author)

During 1991, possibly as the result of fire damage to several of the older units, at least two 2-car diesel railcar sets were transferred to Majorca from lines in Northern Spain, where they had been displaced by electrification. These vehicles had been built by MAN in 1984, and carry running numbers in the 2300 series. Painted in the new white/yellow FEVE livery, they are providing much of the daily basic services, although at least two of the earlier railcars and six trailers are still available in reserve.

The Diesel Locomotives.

During the final years of steam operation up to the final withdrawal of freight services there were four 675 hp B-B type diesels at work on the system. They had been built at Bilbao by the Sociedad Española de Construccion Naval under license from Krupp, and arrived in 1959. Numbers 1101- 1103 went into service straight away, while number 1104 was in use the following year. They weighed 52 tonnes and were painted ESTADO two-tone green. Initially they were used for mixed traffic work but proved to be very heavy on fuel and prone to derailment, though this could have been due to the state of the permanent way which they tended to damage even when staying on the rails. After the end of freight services and the closure of the Santany and Felanitx branches there was little for them to do. Two were quickly sent back to the mainland and while the other pair could be seen laid up at Palma as late as 1974, they too were eventually transferred.

Another type of diesel locomotive has been running on the FC de Mallorca since 1981. This is a metre gauge six-coupled diesel shunter built by Batignolles-Chatillon/CAF in 1960. It carries the running number 1207 and is painted in the all-blue FEVE style.

Other Motive Power.

Various other items have been employed from time to time on the system, especially in connection with the conversion of the railway to metre gauge. At different times since 1981 a Matisa ballast tamper, a Plasser track tester and an unidentified self-propelled rail-lorry have been sighted, all painted in Vias y Obras (p.w. dept.) yellow livery. With the completion of the gauge conversion they appear to have been transferred elsewhere. In earlier years the V y O department owned a selection of powered work trolleys which do not appear to have survived the change of gauge. Two were built at Palma in the 1950s and were based at Llubi and Santa Maria, while another pair were kept at Lluchmajor and Manacor. In later years two Fordson road tractors were used to position wagons on the Palma dockside sidings, presumably collecting them from the waterfront classification sidings where they had been left by one of the larger locomotives after the retirement of the 0-4-0Ts.

Finally, another vehicle was formerly in use on the railway, this being a Renault inspection "draisine" similar to one formerly used on the FC de Soller. In fact it was built in the Soller's workshops in about 1930 for the use of the manager of the FC de Mallorca, who used it to travel between Palma and his estate at Arta. Painted brown, it was derelict but still in evidence inside the Palma roundhouse in the late 1970s.

Matisa ballast tamper at work at Consell y Alaró in 1981.   (Author)

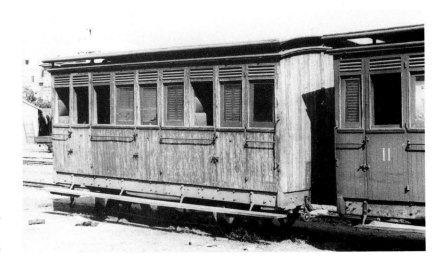

1st class carriage No 39
and Correo/2nd coach.
(Michael Andress)

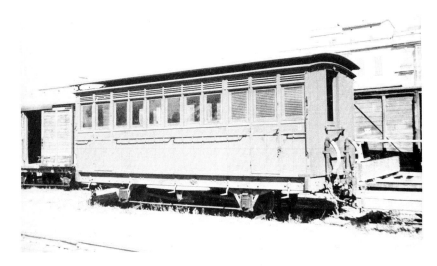

1st class saloon carriage
No 3.   (Mike Swift)

Bogie composite carriage
built by Material Móvil y
Construcciones. (Author)

Chapter 4
The Rolling Stock of The FC de Mallorca

Passenger Vehicles

The first coaches obtained for the opening of the line came from Brown Marshall of Birmingham. They were four-wheeled compartment vehicles offering Preferente (1st Class) and General (2nd Class) accommodation. Shortly afterwards the railway appears to have obtained five other 2nd Class coaches, possibly of the "toast-rack" type, though these seem to have been laid aside from December 1877, perhaps when another batch of new carriages arrived from England. Third Class carriages also feature in Brown Marshall's designs and these must have been introduced before the end of the century; however it was not until the concession for the Santany line was granted that the railway was obliged to cater for this class. The earliest carriages had wooden underframes, and as designed had fully panelled sides, though they may have been supplied with matchboarding lower panels, in which condition the survivors were photographed in the 1950s. A second roof was fitted to protect the occupants from the sun's heat. Livery was brown. More carriages were added over the years, including a single six-wheeled coach. Despite its Cleminson wheel arrangement this seems to have been a problem vehicle, prone to minor derailments. One batch of coaches were built by the Swansea Wagon Co. in 1878 . Among these later arrivals were some passenger brake vans which had been omitted from the initial order. These almost always had birdcage lookouts, except for one variety, built by Brown Marshall, which had duckets instead. In all 60 coaches were used on the main line as well as the branches to La Puebla and Felanitx.

Because of the war, the company had to approach CAF (Beasain) to supply sixteen assorted carriages for the Santany line. These had steel underframes, and included some rather spartan Brake/Thirds whose passenger compartments only had windows in the doors. In some of them the compartment at the opposite end from the Guard was a Postal compartment with a letterbox. An earlier design of Postal coach, used on the main line, had a central mail section with a 2nd Class compartment at each end. This type of coach was often used as a trailer by the De Dion railcars on the Felanitx services. The Santany line coaches were numbered in a separate list to the main line stock. By 1960 twenty nine main line and six Santany four wheeled coaches were still in service, but these were retired when the B-B diesels took over passenger services.

During the 1930s fourteen luxurious bogie carriages were provided by Carde y Escoriaza. These had vestibule ends with wrought iron balconies as well as central doors, and came in two varieties - First/Second composite and all Second Class. The last survivor, number 107, is a composite and shows that the three First Class compartments, whose well padded seats are upholstered in moquette, had a tiny side corridor giving access to a toilet next to the centre door. At the other end of the coach the Second Class compartment was a saloon fitted with comfortable armchairs, though others of this type had two seats either side of a central walkway. This accomodation was so far superior to the normal Seconds that a supplementary fare was payable for its use. The composites were numbered 101-108, while the Seconds were numbers 109-114. The new coaches weighed around 20 tonnes, but carried fewer passengers than the FC de Soller bogie carriages which weighed some 5 tonnes less. This lack of capacity was partly remedied by relocating the Second Class seating at the end of the 1950s, providing an extra 18 places in the all Seconds and 8 more in the Composites.

Brake Vans

Apart from coaches with Guard's accommodation, there were eventually 32 brake vans which were used on both passenger and goods services, though their construction was more akin to goods vehicles, with horizontal planking and vertical metal angle strapping. These arrived at various times from 1876, and again there were several minor design variations. All had a birdcage lookout at one end, central sliding doors giving access to a goods compartment with a capacity of 3 tonnes, and a small dog-box with a barred door in the van side - this probably fitted below the raised floor of the brakeman's lookout. These vehicles numbered in the F series (Furgón = Brake van), though there were also 7 S-series brake vans which were built at Palma for the Santany line. Later in the 1930s three of the Santany line's 3rd Class coaches were rebuilt as brake vans, with vertical

De Dion railcar with blue and white trailer coaches for Santany and Arenal waits to depart from Palma, 21st February 1955. (Brian Butt)

E-class brake van. (Michael Andress)

matcboard bodies, and these were given E series numbers. As they had end doors and fall-plates they must have been used with the new bogie carriages to allow access for the Ticket Inspectors.

Goods Stock

The railway was generously provided with wagons, reaching a total of over 600 in the 1930s, including the F-series brake vans. The late 1950s saw numbers drop sharply, almost one hundred wagons being scrapped over a period of six years. After goods traffic ended almost all were scrapped except for a handful of lowsides and flats which have been retained for p.w. work, although not all have yet been converted to metre gauge.

After the initial order, wagons were added from time to time as required by the opening of new lines, and occasionally wagons were imported in "kit" form and assembled by Palma Workshops. Apart from Brown Marshall, the railway also patronised Swansea Wagon Co, Lancaster Wagon Co, and Pickering's who supplied the last British-built wagons in 1913. By this time European builders had begun to supply the company and after 1914 CAF (Beasain) became the main supplier of rolling stock, though Palma Workshops built about 70 wagons in the 1920s.

By the 1930s the railway owned 139 high sided open wagons, 173 dropside wagons, 184 vans, 22 cattle trucks, 6 bolsters, 2 bogie and 49 four-wheeled flat trucks. This list was augmented by a hearse wagon and two brakedown vans, fitted out to deal with minor accidents. The earliest wagons were fitted with vertical brake standards and a seat for the brakeman (84 opens and 56 vans). The rest were given traditional brake levers.

Series A. Open wagons (1-98, 150-174, 201-216)

These were originally a Brown Marshall design having bow ends, diagonal planking and outside wooden bracing. Cupboard-style doors were fitted. Another variant had sides of five horizontal planks with metal angle bracing. Of the total, 42 had screw brakes, the remainder having brake levers. The axle boxes were joined with a tie-bar and had small W-irons; the wheelbase was 2.133m. External body length was 3.963m and the sides were 0.915m high. The bow ends were 3.963m high and 1.980m wide. The A-series were mainly used for coal traffic.

Series B. Drop-side wagons (1-140, 301-333)

These two-plank dropside wagons were used for the carriage of general goods. Pictures show them loaded with manure, bundles of timber (possibly firewood), stone building blocks, and also in the case of B41 a cylindrical tank for weedkiller.

Originally the series started as a Brown Marshall design with the same general dimensions as the A-series vehicles. (including numbers B27 and B30). Later examples built by CAF Beasain retained the vertical brake at first but lengthened the chassis to 5.180m with a wheelbase measuring 2.490m. A total of 131 were fitted with brake levers acting on one wheel on one side of the wagon only; the remainder had screw brakes.

Series C. Goods Vans. (1-132, 150-174, 201-227)

In the railway's earliest years no brake vans were provided and the goods vans performed this function, only two of them being recorded as general freight carriers in the Annual Report of 1877. The original design was for a 12-plank vehicle with outside wooden bracing and a sliding door on each side. A sample number of this original style is C86. The body is unusual in being as wide as it was high - these were low vehicles so as to give sufficient headroom for a brakeman seated on the roof. Another variation is a low bodied van with a brake lever as typified by vans C57, C80 and C97.

Yet another style of van is shown by C9 and C158, both high bodied vans of nineteen planks whose brakeman's seat was let into the bodywork so that the brake handle just clears the peak of the roof. In addition there was a ventilation hatch covered by a vertically sliding metal plate to the left of the door. There is also a high bodied variant with a solebar brake lever. At least one of this group had no hatch (C27), while another had a narrow hatch with two bars but no metal cover plate. Fifty six of the vans had screw brakes, while the rest had brake levers at solebar level.

All the C-series vans were built on the short chassis with the smaller axle box W-irons. In addition to these vehicles, two more vans were fitted out with emergency equipment for use in case of derailments.

One of the later vans with a brakeman's seat let into the bodywork.
(J-L Rochais, courtesy of J. Wiseman)

B-class wagon No B41 with tank.
(Michael Andress)

The small crane truck outside the workshops at Palma. (Michael Andress)

Series D. Cattle wagons. (1-22)

These vans had semi-open bodies with 15 horizontal slats each approximately 75mms wide separated by gaps measuring 50mms. Vertical strapping was metal angle and there were diagonal bracing bars below waist height. They were 5.10 metres in length.

Series P,R and T. Flat wagons. (P1-4, 11-12; R1-2; T1-49)

These three classes were all flat wagons, though the Ps had a single swivelling bolster at one time, later removed. Early wagons had the short chassis (P6 was a late survivor), while P1, 3, 5 and 11 were the long wheelbase variety. P3 was later fitted out as a weedkilling wagon with discharge tanks and a pump mechanism and still survives. The two R series vehicles were unique as they were the only bogie goods wagons on the island. Their main dimensions are: body length 7.620m, bogie centres 4.570m, bogie wheelbase 1.220m, wheel diameter 0.760m. The width of the wagon is 2 metres. A brake lever is fitted to each bogie, the lever projecting towards the wagon's centre with the pivot and crank working the brake shoes being on the outer end of the bogie frames. A line of four ring bolts along the side frame enable the load to be roped down for transit. R1 (still with 3ft gauge wheels) was still at Palma in 1984.

Other Rolling Stock:

Crane truck

A small crane built by Tangye of Birmingham was mounted on a very short flat wagon and used around the yard at Palma to unload goods and stores. No couplings were fitted.

Hearse Wagon.

This seems to have been converted from a goods van. It was painted black and was lined with fringed black velvet inside, with four large candlesticks at the corners of the bier. When needed it was run in a special train along with a carriage for the mourners and a brake van. No fare was charged for its use.

Rolling Stock Imported From Other Lines.

Since FEVE took over the running of the railway several items of rolling stock have been imported:-

Hopper wagons.

Four of these metre gauge wagons were brought to Majorca from the FC Sierra Menera for the ballasting of the new metre gauge track. One subsequently suffered a broken axle and has been laid aside, while the others have been given a coat of yellow paint since their arrival at Palma.

Tool Coach.

Also belonging to the Brigada de Vias y Obras (p.w. dept.) is a clerestory bogie coach. In 1981 this still retained its original dark though somewhat faded green livery with a yellow stripe below the windows, but by 1984 it too had received a coat of yellow paint with black warning chevrons at each end, together with steel plates or heavy metal mesh protecting the side windows. The inside has been gutted making it suitable for a mobile tool store. Originally this coach formed part of an electric multiple unit on the Valencian suburban system.

Open Wagon

Finally there is an odd open wagon, number M10, which carries no other identifying marks. It is totally unbraked and the body sits much higher on its running gear than any of the other wagons. The couplings have been lowered to match the rest of the stock.

A Note on Couplings

The FC de Mallorca has always used "chopper" style couplings whose centre line is set at 0.670m above rail height. The top of the hook is swept back into a loop which provides a convenient grip when coupling up. In addition there was originally a light chain about 30cms in length, with a small round weight at the end, hanging from the shank of each coupling. Side chains were also provided.

KEY TO STATION LAYOUT PLANS

A	Staff Accommodation	C	Coaling Stage	CL	Coal Wharf	CS	Carriage Shed
D	Dwelling	E	Engine Shed	F	Forge	G	Goods Shed
H	Hotel	Ind	Industrial Buildings	K	Kiosk	L	Loading Platform
O	Offices	P	Pointsman's Hut	PTA	Prefabricated Track Assembly Area		
R	Railcar Shed	S	Shed/store	SB	Station Building	T	Toilets
TS	Tram Shed	V	Permanent Way Department			W	Water Tank/column
WR	Railcar Washer	X	Crossing Keeper's hut			Y	Yard Office

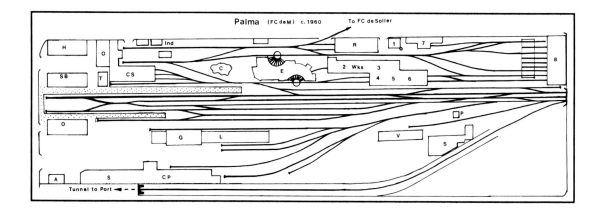

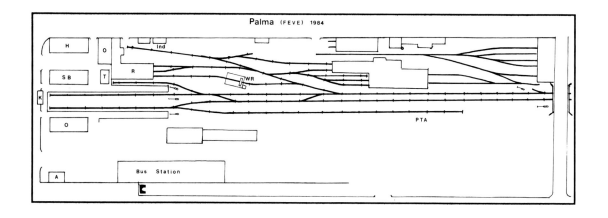

Chapter 5
The Route Described

Today's train traveller leaving Palma will find the stations of both the island's railways situated in the Plaza España. The old FC de Mallorca station has two platforms formerly shaded by plane trees now pruned to a fraction of their earlier shape. Both platforms are flanked by matching single storey buildings, that on the eastern platform (vía 1) housing the offices of the various operating departments. The western platform (vía 2) has a short bay along part of one side (vía 3). The building on this side of the station includes the General Waiting Room, Booking Office and the office of the Jefe de Estación (Station Master). Both structures have hipped roofs with acanthus leaf decorations on the corners of the eaves. Walls are whitewashed and the woodwork of the doorways and window shutters is painted green. Also on the western side is a separate toilet building tucked in behind the carriage shed which spans three roads flanking the bay platform. In former days each of the longer platforms had an engine release line which met to form two linked tracks in the centre of the station. These lines were often left full of goods vehicles and partly made up trains during the less busy times of the day, when mule carts were driven across the tracks to unload directly from the newly arrived goods wagons.

The western side of the station yard was once almost wholly taken up by the facilities for servicing and maintaining the line's motive power and rolling stock. Until its demolition c.1980 there was a double roundhouse served by twin turntables. This has been replaced by running sheds for the railcars, behind which a single line runs through the workshop yard. At one time there was a gateway in the adjacent wall and a siding provided access to the tracks of the FC de Soller in the street outside. Also, in earlier times there was a siding running parallel to the main line which served an industrial complex beyond the station throat, while the Santany branch provided the fourth of the lines at the station throat. Until the cessation of freight traffic, the goods yard filled the eastern side of the station layout though today the capacious goods shed, now devoid of tracks, is the only reminder of this activity.

At the outermost end of the goods yard a trailing connection off the Santany branch led to a single line which, once parallel to the nearby road, began a steep descent vanishing into the tunnel that eventually brought the tracks onto the dockside just to the east of the Cathedral. Today the seaward end of this tunnel is closed by locked gates. A nice touch is provided above the tunnel mouth by a relief carving of one of the Nasmyth Wilson 4-4-0 tank engines hauling a train of vans. This medallion is garlanded by carved fruit and plaques giving the construction date, 1932. The spoil from the tunnel was originally used to reclaim part of the foreshore where a marshalling yard consisting of five parallel loop tracks was laid out. At one time a passenger station was planned here, but this never materialised, presumably falling a victim to the recession following the Civil War. Beyond the loops, the line split to serve the southern and eastern wharves of the main harbour where a triangle of lines was provided to turn the larger locomotives which could now serve the port. Such was the steam era layout of the capital's terminus. The advent of diesel railcars together with the end of goods traffic brought about various subtle changes in the 3ft gauge as certain tracks became disused and vanished under the ballast which over the years had become a compacted mixture of stone, earth and coal dust covering the sleepers to rail-top height. The engine release lines between the platforms were simplified and most of the goods yard was lost beneath the site of the new bus station. However the most radical change was caused by the decision to widen the line to metre gauge. This caused a wholesale sweeping away of all traces of the former layout and the demolition of the old steam roundhouses, which photographs taken in 1979 show had fallen into rather a ruinous state. Work seems to have started in 1980 and by the following year the basics of the new formation were nearing completion, although train services were still being worked by 3ft gauge stock. The site of the goods yard was covered with a huge heap of old rails lifted from around the yard and out along the main line to Inca, and where the goods yard headshunt had been a short length of unconnected 3 foot gauge track provided a resting place for the last surviving F-class brake van.

Three years later a further visit found the metre gauge well established, and the station layout complete apart from the line through the workshops which was still laid with derelict 3 foot gauge track. A carriage washer had been built on one approach road to the carriage shed (vía 6) while a kick-back siding from vía 1 now

The station building on platform2 at Palma.   (Author)

Krupp-built 2-6-0T No 31 shunting at Santa Maria.   (D. Trevor Rowe)

served a construction area for pre-fabricated trackwork complete with tower cranes and large stocks of new rails and sleepers. The self propelled track testing vehicles and rail lorries seen on the previous trip were still in evidence. By now all trains were running on the metre gauge line, now doubled for about half the distance to Inca. Trains could use both tracks as far as Santa Maria although beyond here only one line was operational. Trains were crossing at Santa Maria, and though loops had also been provided at Consell y Alaró and Lloseta these did not seem to be in use.

For the first time in the railway's history comprehensive signalling had been introduced with three aspect electric signals giving Red (Danger), Green (All Clear) and Blue/white (Shunt Ahead) indications. Control of the station's turnouts remained as ground throw levers beside the lines, although a new pattern of switch was in use, somewhat similar to those in use on the FC de Soller.

PALMA TO INCA

(In the following descriptions the use of the words Right, Left, Down, Facing and Trailing all apply to trains travelling from Palma towards the outer terminus.)

The present journey between Palma and Inca, while being of some interest to the narrow gauge fan, has only limited appeal for the railway historian. The gauge conversion coming on top of over fifteen years of operation by diesel railcars has wiped away many of the original features of the line; however echoes of the past can still be picked up here and there.

The initial run out of Palma is arrow straight through the industrialised suburbs of the capital. At Pont D'Inca (4 kms) the former branch to Santany turned off to the right on a south easterly course, and after the station a more curved section of track is encountered as far as Marratxi (9 kms). From here a gentle, but none the less steady climb starts that reaches the summit of 158 metres just beyond Consell y Alaró. After Marratxi, Santa Maria (14 kms) was the first important stop, as it was the junction of the line to Felanitx. In steam days there were three tracks through the station, the centre one being used by goods trains during shunting moves to allow following passenger trains to overtake. Today the two running lines pass straight through, although there are cross-overs provided at each end of the station.

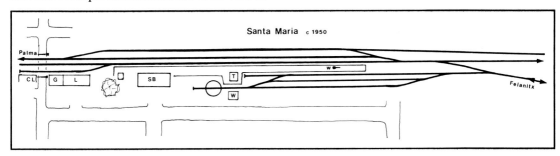

The next station, Consell (19 kms), was once the junction for the line serving Alaró which closed in 1935. The present layout includes a loop serving a new island platform on the Down line, the Up line passing straight through in front of the station building. From here the track falls slightly towards the next stop at Binisalem (22 kms), now no more than a couple of platforms on either side of the line together with a refurbished station building. For most of the journey so far the railway and the road have kept relatively close company. Now they separate, the railway running through an area of fruit trees to reach the town of Lloseta (26 kms) which has the usual two-storey station building and a loop line similar to the one at Consell.

INCA.

The railway enters Inca (29 kms) on a right hand curve from the west. The Palma end of the yard is marked by a level crossing recently provided with modern automatic barriers. The station building is still as shown in old photographs but the island platform is a new one, higher and shorter than the previous example. The layout is now extremely simple, the Down line splitting into a loop embracing the island platform opposite the old station building, and there are a couple of sidings for stabling spare rolling stock. Beyond the platform

The restored station at Binisalem in 1984 shows how the building must have looked almost a century earlier. (Author)

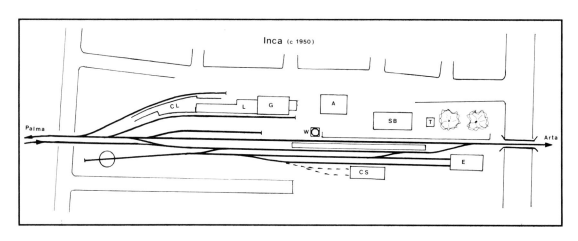

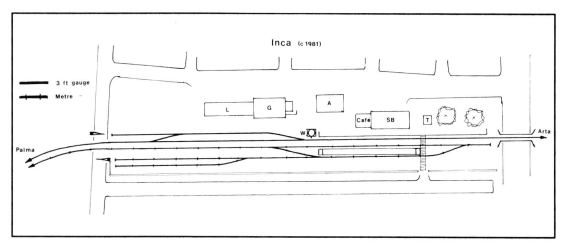

MTM 2-6-0 No 7 and train at Inca in 1957. The station clock shows the time as 10.00, so the train is almost certainly bound for La Puebla. (D. Trevor Rowe)

Railcars awaiting their next turn of duty at Inca in 1977. (K. Taylorson)

MAJORCA RAILWAYS INCA GOODS SHED

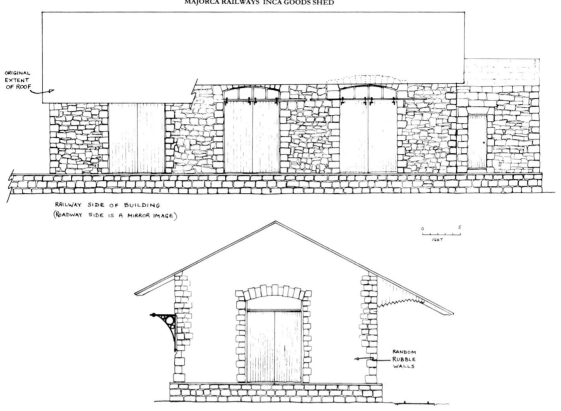

ORIGINAL
EXTENT
OF ROOF

RAILWAY SIDE OF BUILDING
(ROADWAY SIDE IS A MIRROR IMAGE)

RANDOM
RUBBLE
WALLS

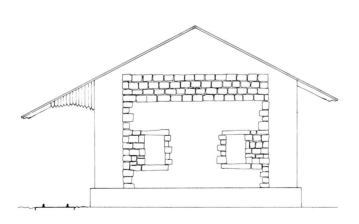

the line makes a physical connection with the remains of the 3ft gauge rails that continue on from here into the centre of the island.

In the steam era Inca was a more important station. Trains to Manacor and La Puebla were sometimes combined and double headed as far as here. They were then split to run ahead as two separate workings. There was a goods yard on the left of the line while opposite were a couple of sidings which served, in the early days at least, a carriage shed and an engine shed, though these may have fallen out of use before the end of the steam era. At the Down end of the platform the surrounding land falls away and the railway runs onto a stone embankment. Beyond this is an arched stone bridge which carries the single line across the street below. The tracks continue in a south easterly direction and cross the town's new by-pass on a modern girder bridge at the edge of the built-up area.

<h2 style="text-align:center">THE OLD MAIN LINE (now closed)</h2>

EMPALME.

Beyond Inca the line runs through farmland to Empalme, the junction of the branch to La Puebla. It appears that the station was only provided for railway interchange, as there is no official public road serving the station, which can only be reached along a track leading to a large farm - the Son Bordils estate that gave the station its original name. A couple of hundred metres beyond the old farmhouse the lane terminates on a goods loading bank opposite the station. While the station name conjours up mental pictures of an oasis, the fact is that in Spanish the word Empalme merely means Junction.

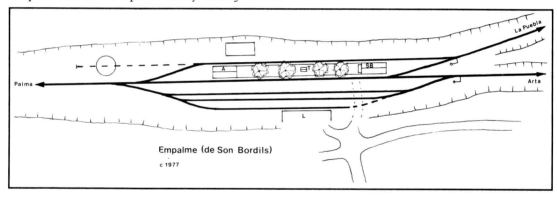

Empalme (de Son Bordils)
c 1977

Wintery trees add to the desolation of Empalme in 1988. The track layout was still complete and the buildings in a reasonable state of preservation some eight years after the last train.   (Author)

The layout at Empalme (34 kms) differs from the other stations on the system. The single line from Inca splits into several parallel loops and the isolated platform is situated between the two left hand tracks. The platform has a two storey building at each end, both built in a simple country style unlike anything on the line built previously. The station house nearer the lane was used by the stationmaster and there is the remains of a garden between the tracks with a well for drinking water. Plane trees shade the platform and the tiny building which housed the toilets. Near the Inca end of the running loops are the foundations of a water tank, an ashpit and the well of an old turntable.

Beyond the station the two loops split to form the diverging lines which vanish into roughly parallel rocky cuttings, the line to Manacor being straight and on a falling gradient; after emerging from the far end of the hill it runs on an embankment across the semi-wooded countryside towards Sineu. The La Puebla branch curves round to the left and runs generally north east to reach the next station, Llubi.

THE ARTA LINE (closed 1977)

SINEU.

After Empalme the main line enters an area of low rolling hills, which force the railway to change direction a number of times before reaching the outskirts of Sineu. Here two roads are crossed in quick succession, the places formerly protected by crossing keepers who were provided with small wooden shelters, now vanished. The station (43 kms) is a little more generous than usual. A loop opens up on the right and a former facing siding (now lifted) served the goods shed, which still stands next to the station. On the far side of the main line was a second shorter loop line that once served a coal wharf. As with many other stations there is a narrow island platform between the running lines, opposite the station building which dates from the 1920s.

Beyond the platform the loops combine to form the single line that continues on towards Manacor. At this end of the station there is a level crossing with barriers that were once worked by a winch situated beside the station house. Just before the crossing on the left of the line stands a small smithy built of sandstone blocks. Leaving the town the line runs into a shallow, wooded cutting and shortly after the road linking Sineu and Petra passes over the line.

P.W. DEPT. HUT SINEU

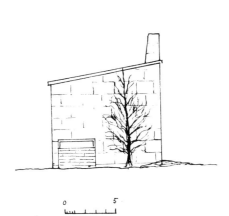

0 5
FEET

SANDSTONE BLOCKS WITH REMAINS OF THIN CEMENT RENDERING
DOOR, WINDOW FRAMES AND COAL BIN : WEATHERED WOOD

INTERIOR : ROUGH STONE BLOCK FLOOR. HEARTH FOR
BLACKSMITH WORK IN REAR CORNER. RUSTY TOOLS.

Sineu station showing the canopy over the platform. (Author)

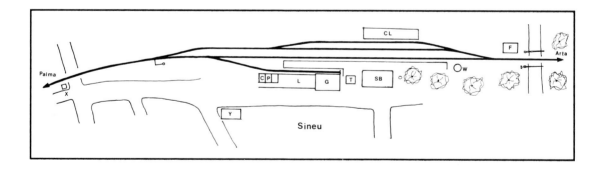

SAN JUAN.

The station at San Juan (43 kms) does not appear on the map of the island as it has been converted into a private dwelling. The line at this point is on a steadily falling gradient and there was originally a loop by the platform with a facing siding running into the goods shed. The loop was later lifted. The modest station building has no upper floor. Passing on, the line swings round to run east once more, as the countryside becomes more mountainous and wooded. Eventually the land flattens out and fields once again border the line.

PETRA

The station buildings at Petra (54 kms) are finished in a rougher more rural style than Sineu, but there are the normal three doorways leading off the platform, the station name being carved on a plaque over the centre door. The stonework, like Sineu, is randomly shaped with only the corner stones and lintels being squared off. However, where Sineu is built mainly of roughly similar hexagonal blocks, here the stones are much more random giving the walls the appearance of an old Chinese vase whose surface glaze is covered with minute cracks. At the Palma end of the platform a row of magnificent plane trees once provided shade for any waiting passengers. Today the layout at Petra merely consists of a long loop of track opposite the platform. However the presence of the goods shed just beyond the station house shows there was once a goods siding too, and that unusually it faced away from Palma.

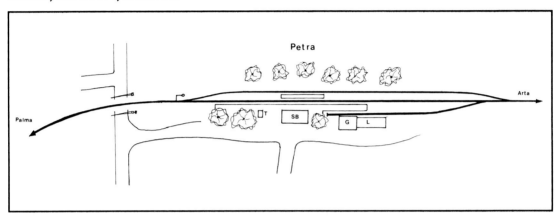

Petra station in 1981, some years after closure.   (Author)

48

After Petra the countryside becomes more rocky as the railway breaks through a line of hills in its path. Beyond them the railway meets the main road at a level crossing once protected by lifting barriers which have now been removed. The cottage for the crossing attendant remains however, and is still inhabited, although road re-surfacing has covered the rails with asphalt.

The street facade of the goods shed at Petra displays the simple lines of the local architecture; note the crane at the far end of the building.   (Author)

MANACOR

Approaching from the west the line opens out into a long loop at the edge of the town, and there is a stone built shelter, now in ruins, for the pointsman on duty here. On the right hand side is a large factory once provided with a trailing siding, beyond which formerly stood the goods shed, now replaced by modern housing. After this comes the station platform which originally ran parallel to the station building. The later extension to Arta needed to thread its way along existing alleyways in the town and caused a slight re-alignment curving away from the old building.

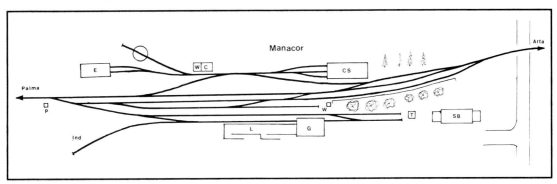

A view of the old platform at Manacor; in later times the railway was relaid to the photographer's left.
(Author)

At the Palma end of the station is the ruin of the two track engine shed with the remains of the water tank and coaling stage nearby, and most of the tracks have been lifted except for those serving the platform. At the Arta end of the station there is an old two aspect colour light signal and also a tiny stone hut for the attendant responsible for the level crossing over one of the main roads through the town. On the far side the line runs between two old houses, and then traverses another intersection of minor roads before curving to the right along an unmade street. At a final level crossing the railway leaves the town and sets off through the surrounding farmland in an easterly direction.

MAJORCA RAILWAYS CROSSING KEEPER'S COTTAGE (NEAR MANACOR)

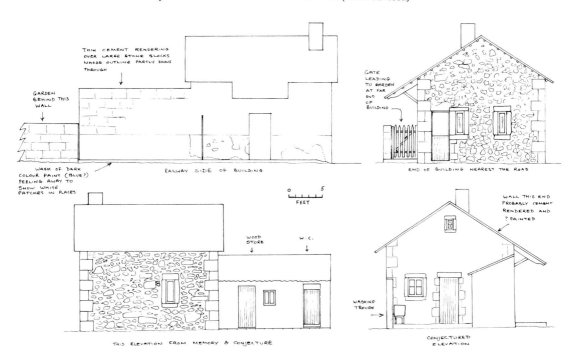

SAN LORENZO.

By the time the line reaches San Lorenzo (78 kms) it is some twenty metres above the level of the town and the station is situated on a shelf cut out of the hillside. A short facing siding serves the goods shed, and the less intensive service on this section of the railway is reflected by the lack of the extra platform between the two sides of the loop.

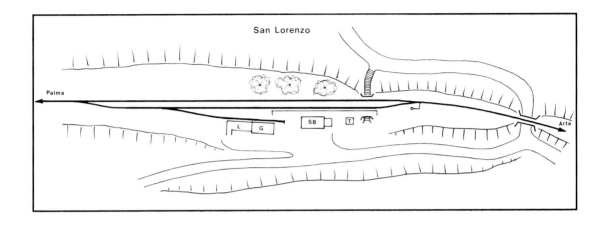

The roadway facade of the station at San Lorenzo. (Author)

MAJORCA RAILWAYS SAN LORENZO GOODS SHED

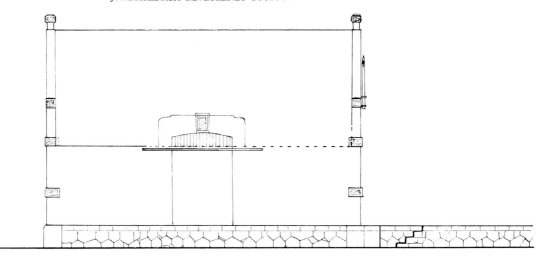

RAILWAY SIDE OF BUILDING

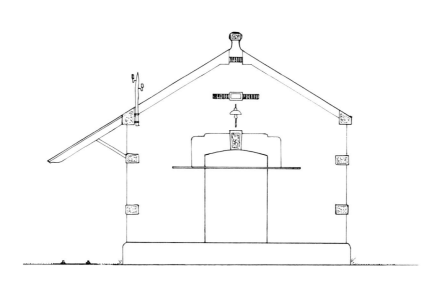

FEET

METRES

San Lorenzo goods shed. (Author)

SAN LORENZO GOODS SHED

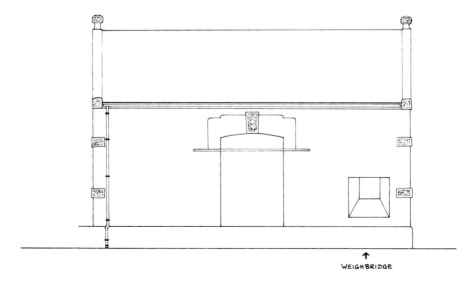

WEIGHBRIDGE

0   5   10   FEET

0   1   2   3   METRES

SAN MIGUEL.

After San Lorenzo the land is more wooded and there is a short tunnel to negotiate in this stretch. The railway changes direction yet again to reach the small town of San Miguel from where there was once a plan to build a branch line to serve nearby Porto Cristo and the Caves of Drach. The station buildings have a pleasant rural style characterised by the rather lumpy stone plinths at the ends of the roof ridges which are a typical feature of the buildings of the Arta extension. The design is somewhat redeemed by the decorative red and white tile decoration applied to the gable ends. The track layout latterly consisted of a goods loop opposite the platform with no freight facilities apart from the remains of a loading bank, though there was once a facing siding south of the station platform.

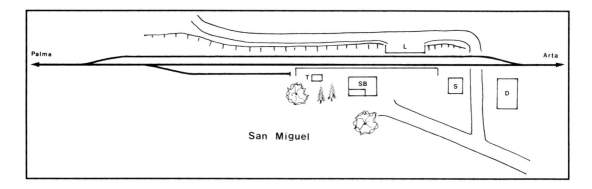

A general view of San Miguel. (Author)

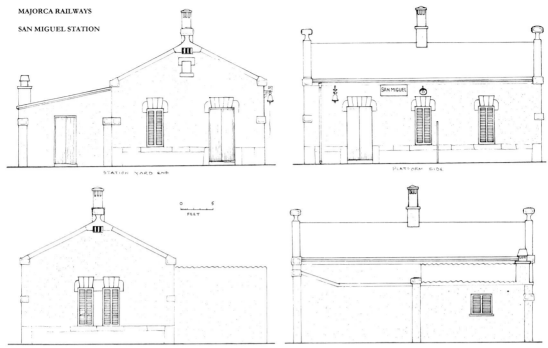

MAJORCA RAILWAYS

SAN MIGUEL STATION

STATION YARD END

PLATFORM SIDE

0   5
FEET

STIPPLED AREA : GRITTY PEBBLEDASH - PROBABLY PAINTED A FADED YELLOW-OCHRE COLOUR
STONEWORK : VERY PALE GREY .   RED/WHITE STRIPED TILES AT GABLE ENDS
DOORS + WINDOW TRIM : VERY PALE GREEN (EAU-DE-NIL)

Typical bridge architecture on the FC de Mallorca. This one is located between San Miguel and Son Servera.
(Author)

SON SERVERA.

Beyond San Miguel the line is carried on an embankment above the fields for some distance and the line turns northward again to reach Son Servera (84 kms), where the station is situated in a cutting below the town. As usual there is a loop line opposite the platform and a facing siding on the left of the line which serves a loading bank and goods shed, the latter shaded by a luxuriant palm tree.

At the edge of the town a minor road is crossed, and the farmland soon gives way to a hilly woodland with rocky outcrops. Some two kilometres further on there is a rather sudden level crossing which must have needed a full-time attendant as there is a wooden hut nearby. The line continues through the woods and reappears to cross the road once more. This section also includes another short tunnel and a bridge over a dried up river bed.

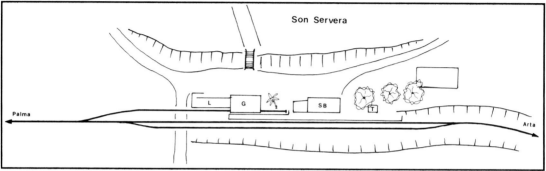

ARTA.

Nearing journey's end and still climbing, the railway approaches Arta, swinging round to approach from the west. A warning of the nearby town is provided by the local cemetery whose access road provides yet another level crossing. Ahead the town now comes into view. A final level crossing carries the line over a side street which crosses the line just beyond the running sheds. On the right of the line trailing turnouts (now lifted) gave access to the two road carriage shed, while opposite is the two road engine shed, also now devoid of tracks and today used by a stonemason. The bricked up doorways at the far end of the building once led to the turntable.

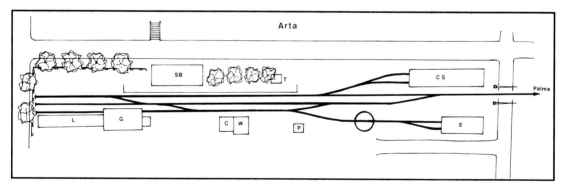

Opposite the platform two loops open up on the left. The outermost one serves the combined water tank and coal store, and here there is an ashpit between the rails. The turntable and engine shed tracks were reached by setting back from here, although these rails have now been lifted or obscured by buildings. Beyond the water tank a facing crossover allows access to the headshunt at the inner end of the yard, while the straight track continues as the goods shed siding. The passenger platform is shaded by pine trees whose cones litter the ground while the station house is a tall building much embellished with coping stones which project from its rendered walls. Behind the station the roadway rises up parallel to the line, which ends at a sheer stone wall a short distance beyond the platform, 94 kilometres from Palma.

Arta Engine shed. The doorway is a new addition since closure. Originally locomotives entered the building from the opposite end.   (Author)

Arta station.   (Author)

THE LA PUEBLA BRANCH (closed 1981)

LLUBI.

Llubi is the first stop on the branch after Empalme, and in true narrow gauge style the station is some distance from the village which perches on a hilltop above a neighbouring valley. Llubi (39 kms) has a simple layout and looks as if it had been downgraded to halt status in later years. The station house is a single-storey building without frills and the platform is protected by a row of cypress trees. The garden formerly belonging to the stationmaster was once shaded by an arbour of vines and there was once a loop line opposite the platform though this was taken out some time ago. The single facing siding was left in place and serves a loading bank which must have been the scene of much activity once, judging by the Freight Consignment book for 1939-1941 discovered in a nearby store. Most freight was weighed, presumably in the station Parcels Office before being loaded (and sometimes stored) in wagons or vans awaiting dispatch. Two or three wagon loads a day seem to have been the average plus several small consignments that probably travelled in the brake van.

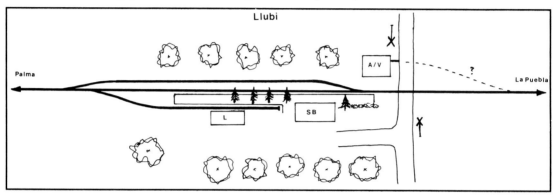

Where the narrow road from the village crosses the line, road users were protected from the trains by lengths of chain that could be slung between red and white painted posts beside the tracks. Beside the line is a large stone building which has a set of rails protruding from its doors leading off the road. From the shape of a small field opposite it is possible that this was once part of a trailing siding. In 1981 the building contained a small motorised platelayer's trolley and some tools, but these were later removed. The upper floor had once provided staff living quarters.

Llubi station, taken three
months after closure.
(Author)

MURO.

Like Llubi, the village of Muro is some two kilometres away from the railway, though here the traffic must have been greater as the facilities are more generous. Approaching from the junction trains emerge onto an area of open ground and there is an ungated crossing of a minor road, marked by the usual X-shaped sign. From here the railway runs across a slight embankment towards a rocky hillock which it penetrates by means of a cutting. Meanwhile the nearby road climbs the hillock to cross the line by a stone arched bridge, before skirting the station and then turning off towards the town.

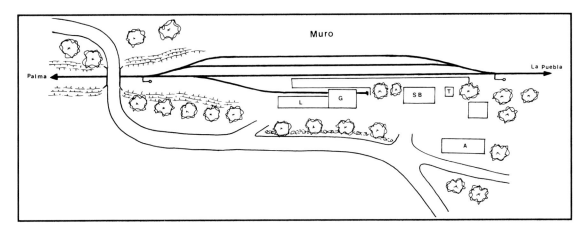

As the tracks emerge from the cutting under the road bridge a loop opens up on the left of the line and the point levers at each end are fitted with indicator discs to warn approaching drivers which way the road is set. The platform is on the right hand side and is shaded by pine trees which separate it from the goods shed which was once served by a facing siding behind the platform. These lines are still in place although the connecting turnout has been lifted. Opposite the platform is the marker showing the distance to Palma, 42.4 kilometres. On the far side of the loop are traces of another loop siding that has now vanished under mounds of old ballast and earth.

Muro station in 1981, showing one of the kilometre marker posts. This view is looking towards La Puebla.

(Author)

59

Between Muro and La Puebla the countryside becomes richer and is intensively farmed. The fields are generally rather small, with the soil raked into parallel ridges to aid irrigation from the storage tanks which are dotted about the countryside. These are made of stone blocks rendered with cement, and feed water channels resembling walls with a grooved top. These lead to the various fields where temporary earth channels water the peppers, maize, alfalfa and olives, although all kinds of fruit and vegetables can be found growing in the area. The more prosperous farms, which tend to have larger fields, nowadays employ automatic water sprinklers.

LA PUEBLA.

Having traversed the fields from Muro the railway enters La Puebla (known these days as Sa Pobla) at a wide road junction. Once the lines were protected by chains hung between posts, but road resurfacing since closure has covered the tracks with asphalt. In former times this was open ground with scattered trees, but the enlargement of the town has resulted in the line from here on threading its way between the backs of houses and light industrial buildings to reach the terminus where facilities are simple but adequate. The platform line has a run-round loop and there is a bay platform on the left. This line passes behind an attractive water tank at the end of the platform where there is an ashpit between the rails. At one time the tank had a spout on either side but latterly only the spout at the front was in use. Adjoining the tank whose base housed the pump for water raising, was a small shed. In steam days there was a trailing connection from the bay which led to the turntable and a two road engine shed. Another track led off the turntable and joined the main line at the station throat, although all traces of this have been covered by recent building work.

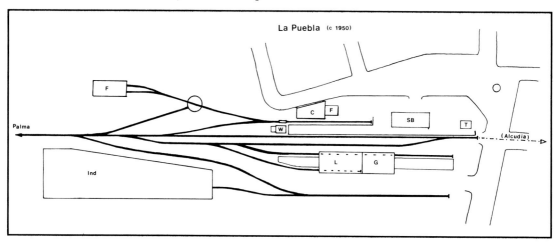

Between the bay platform and the boundary wall is the old coal storage compound and next to it a small hut with a chimney, possibly a forge. Alongside the present loop line is a large warehouse belonging to the Co-operativa Agricola Poblera (the local farmers' co-operative), which was formerly served by its own siding leading off a facing siding for general goods. Between this and the loop line was a siding serving the goods shed and loading bank which was protected by a long canopy. The site of this has now been covered by blocks of apartments built since 1970.

The station building is a long single-storey structure. One end comprises the Booking Hall and Waiting Room, while the rest of the space was occupied by the Stationmaster and his family. The typical shuttered windows and doorways are in evidence, as well as the station bell - still in place a few months after closure, but now removed. The walls of the station were once painted a brownish-maroon, but over the years this had been weathered by the sun to a slightly pinker shade than the original. Around the base of the walls is a strip some 800mm high painted a yellow ochre colour, while the windows and doors, were a very pale shade of green (eau de nil). The station was framed with pine trees which shaded the small courtyard on the street side of the building which was surrounded by a high stone wall with a gateway leading out into the Plaça del Tren. At the far end of the building was a small private garden whose fence was covered in a trailing creeper bearing large purple flowers. This had also climbed onto the roof of the station toilets. The tracks ended without a buffer stop at a gap in the boundary wall opposite an alleyway leading towards the nearby farm produce market, and the map shows that they once may have continued to the far end of the town. This would have been the start of the extension to Alcudia and beyond, had it ever been built, but in the event La Puebla remained as the terminus.

Outside the station the road leading towards the sea provides a bit of local history. It is named Carrer Enginyer Mister Green and recalls the man in charge of draining La Albufera during the mid-nineteenth century. Bidwell, the British Consul on the island during the 1860's, mentions making a detour to view the works. This trip nearly had a tragic ending when his coachman accidentally strayed off the road across the marshland during a torrential storm, and the carriage became bogged down in the mud, almost threatening to sink into the marsh. Luckily the party managed to extricate themselves from the predicament, but the story throws an interesting light on the hazards of travel before the days of the railway.

The water tower at La Puebla.
(Author)

LA PUEBLA WATER TANK

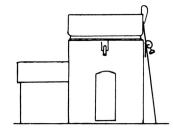 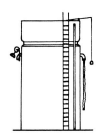 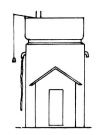 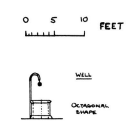

La Puebla station shortly after closure. (Author)

OTHER CLOSED BRANCHES (now lifted)

The foregoing is an account of the lines of the FC de Mallorca which can still be traced with a little patience as they are still in existence although the derelict parts are becoming more hidden with every passing year and have been omitted from the local Firestone map since 1991. To follow the trail of the old lines to Alaró, Santany and Felanitx requires even more patience as in some places the course of the line has vanished completely following the removal of railway embankments to enlarge the neighbouring fields. This is certainly true of the former line to Alaró, closed over fifty years ago. Sometimes an echo remains with the discovery of a crossing keeper's hut, an old bridge or a pathway through the olive trees that is flatter and straighter than a road and yet carries no wheeled traffic.

We have already noted at Santa Maria the old Felanitx line curving away in a south easterly direction. The first stop was **Santa Eugenia** (22 kms) where the station was situated on a curve. The platform was on the right with a loop opposite. Behind the platform a facing siding served a loading bank. After this came **Algaida** (31 kms), whose station layout was almost identical to Santa Eugenia, though with the addition of a goods shed at the end of the single siding. Near the site of the station a crossing keeper's hut survives. Further on at **Montuiri** another hut can be found on the old main road near the bottom of the hill leading up into the town. A short way across the fields is the old station (38 kms), now part of a farm complex, though the station name is still displayed over the doorway. Opposite the platform was the usual loop while the goods siding running in behind the platform here faced toward Felanitx. Despite having no goods shed the station saw plenty of freight traffic, both in full wagon loads as well as small consignments. Where the siding joined the main line there was a water tower, while passengers waiting on the platform were sheltered by the usual plane trees.

Further on at **Porreras** (45 kms) there is still a large, solid two-storey station though traces of the two facing sidings situated behind the platform have disappeared along with the loading bank. Beyond the station is a bridge over the road leading to Campos. In former days unfenced fields of barley bordered this part of the line,

A typical crossing keeper's hut. This one is located at Montuiri. (Author)

— — — — — —

with the crops coming to within a couple of feet of the rails. The next stop was at **Canteras**(51 kms), but the site of this halt is no longer marked on the map. Having crossed a dirt road the line once split to provide a goods loop serving a loading bank, with an additional spur siding facing in each direction. Just beyond the loop was the platform on the right hand side, followed by a second level crossing.

The terminus at **Felanitx** (58 kms) is now hard to recognise, although a large factory on the edge of the town hints at the possibility of a railway. The whole site is now a combination of a scrap dump and a stable yard and in contrast with much of the old remains which have a wistful air, Felanitx seems sad and unloved. In the old days there was a loop line opposite the platform with a couple of sidings on the side of the tracks nearest the town. One of these served the goods shed and the factory may also have had its own loading dock. On the other side of the loop a facing siding ran in beside the engine shed and coal stack. Access to the two-road shed was by a trailing connection off the inner end of the loop, and the turntable was gained from this line, which was also provided with a water tank. There was also a short facing siding running off the inner end of the loop, opposite the station building which has been demolished.

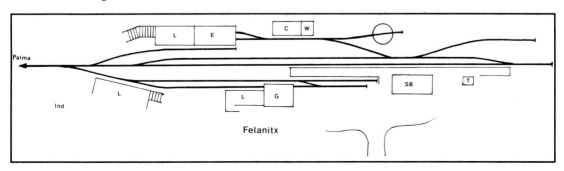

A general view of Arenal looking towards Santany in 1960.   (J.B. Nisbet)

Salinas station showing the site of the original platform.   (Author)

The trail of the former Santany branch is equally elusive, the more so following road building developments in the last few years. Extensions to the airport have covered much of the first few kilometres which used to run through **Coll** (6 kms) and a halt serving the hamlet of **San Francisco** (10 kms). However, driving along the new motorway to Santany an old railway embankment with a low three arch viaduct can be seen on the left hand side a short way east of the airport. The next stop was a halt at **Las Cadenas** (11 kms) where the first house on the edge of the town is a likely candidate for the former station, especially as there is an unpaved road behind it which continues on the other side of the main street, and which could once have been the railway's trackbed.

Further on into **Arenal** itself the site of the line becomes more obvious as it is used as a footpath which uses the high bridge which once took the single track over the deep valley of a small stream. Beyond here new streets and houses have obliterated the course of line, though a straight row of trees betrays the location of the former platform (14 kms) and nearby is an old water tank, now situated in a car park enclosure. Final evidence is provided by the Bar Estación across the road. All this is hard to reconcile with a picture of the station taken shortly before closure. This shows that there was a loop on the left of the line while the station house was on the right hand side; significantly there is no sign of the town in the picture, which looks towards Santany. On the far side of the line there was also a short open platform, while a trailing siding formerly serving a turntable joined the loop opposite the station house. At the far end of the station there was formerly a works producing concrete blocks. Beyond and slightly behind the main platform the water tank can be seen, apparently standing in the goods yard, as further on a large goods shed is visible though the track layout cannot be made out. In the distance the line seems to pass out of sight under an overbridge. There followed a long climb, a substantial viaduct over a dry valley and the marker post for kilometre 17 which was situated in a rocky cutting. The land here was an undulating mixture of woodland and scrub with the line running alternately over embankments and through cuttings. At the summit a long, high curve provided a good view of the Bay of Palma.

A view of the street facade of Santany station in the process of conversion to living accommodation.   (Author)

The town of **Lluchmayor** (30 kms) appears to have sprawled across the railway, though the station was once provided with a double track engine shed capable of stabling four locomotives, and had a generous provision of sidings and loop lines. The next clue that can be picked up is at **Campos** (34 kms) where a crossing-keeper's cottage can be found beside the minor road leading via Ca'n Vaca towards the coast. Further south the line ran through a fertile plain, though traces of the one-time halt at **El Palmer** (48 kms) are hard to find. Further on however at **Banos** (52 kms) the station house still stands in splendid isolation beside the road leading to Ses Salines. Nowadays it is a private dwelling, although it still has the unmistakable features of the Majorcan railway system. The actual baths are some distance away and a bus used to meet the trains which only stopped when the baths were open. New housing seems likely to overtake the station at **Salinas** (55 kms) where the derelict station house and outbuildings still exist just off the main road in the centre of the town. However a picture of the site was seen in the window of an estate agent so re-development may have taken place. Hopefully as the house would make an easy conversion to a dwelling its general outline may be spared, though the same is probably not so true of the other railway structures here. The local industry, which gave the village its name, was the production of salt. This was taken from evaporation beds along the shore, which are still in use today.

Little sign remains of the halt at **Llomparts** (58 kms) which had a three-arched canopy similar to the shelter at San Francisco, but further on at **Santany** (62 kms) most of the railway buildings still exist, although they are now somewhat mixed up with newer houses that have invaded the site, while the station building (or at least the upper floor) has been converted into a dwelling with the addition of an outside staircase. At the outer end of the yard a loop once opened up on the left, and the engine shed on this side and the goods shed on the right once framed the tracks which ran straight ahead into the platform which was on the right hand side of the line. Opposite the platform is a large building, which provided living quarters for the staff, including train crews on overnight lodging turns. On the same side of the line, which by now had opened out into another loop, was the water tank and a raised bank for coaling. Beyond this a turntable provided access to the two tracks running into the engine shed. The line leading straight across the turntable was provided with an inspection pit inside the building, and inside at the rear were two small rooms - perhaps a store/office and a workshop for minor repairs. The whole of the building is now in a very bad state of preservation and may not remain standing much longer.

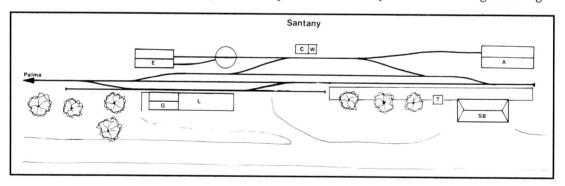

Since closure most of the old buildings have had their doors and ground floor windows sealed with cement breeze blocks. However these have now been pierced and some station interiors show signs of recent vandalism and spray painting which were absent only a short time ago. Decorative features, such as a rather nice ornamental grille in the Ticket Office at San Lorenzo and a handsome cast iron lamp bracket at Empalme have vanished and it seems inevitable that what is left is doomed to a lingering descent into squalor. This is especially sad as the writer's first impression of the old lines in 1981 was of a line asleep. It is now in danger of giving up this shadow of life, and becoming dead indeed.

Chapter 6
Timetables and Train Working

A snapshot of the earliest days of the railway is provided by the Annual Reports which include figures for the average train loading during these years. In 1877 the typical train consisted of three or four of the Composite carriages, a single Second and three or perhaps four goods wagons, mostly with a solitary brake van. Three years later one of the Composites had seemingly been replaced by another brake van in the average formation and the fourth goods wagon had become the rule rather than the exception. Records show that in 1877 none of the locomotives needed to work every day - sometimes remaining unsteamed for as much as ten days a month. That year the three passenger locomotives averaged just over 20,000 kilometres each, compared with the goods locomotives' average of 14,100 kilometres. With a main line round trip of 36 kilometres, and allowing for shunting, an approximate total of 350 goods trips annually can be estimated, while passenger trips work out at about three workings a day.

Indeed for most of its independent life the railway ran a service of three trains on each of the four lines, with departures in the early morning, afternoon and evening being made from the outer termini with corresponding return trips from Palma. Until the doubling of the main line to Inca it was common to work the branches to Felanitx and La Puebla as separate entities, involving a change of train at either Santa Maria or Empalme. Sometimes trains were combined and portions added or detached at the junctions. As the Santany branch left the capital on a separate line its services were worked to and from Palma. From the mid 1930s the railcars came to provide most of the services on the Felanitx and Santany lines. The De Dion cars often towed some of the four-wheeled carriages, and this was certainly a feature of the Summer services on the Santany line, when trains to Arenal were well patronised. Two 3rd class coaches would be added to the train between Palma and Arenal, where one or both trailers would be uncoupled while the railcar continued on to the terminus. Off-season a Correo/2nd class coach was often used to strengthen the railcar services on the two southerly branch lines. In steam days, in addition to the Santany services, there were short Palma-Arenal workings and a turntable was provided at Arenal. These two branch lines would thus have required separate goods workings, whereas the steam-hauled services to La Puebla and Arta were run with mixed trains. Additional goods trains were run on the main line when traffic demanded it, as the time needed for shunting at every wayside station would have been too great to sustain a reliable passenger service, even in more unhurried days. Goods trains tended to leave Palma around mid-day, returning when required; the amount of shunting could mean that the train did not arrive back in Palma until the early hours of the following day.

Until the time that railcars took over most of the train services the FC de Mallorca operated four classes of trains:- Rápidos, Correos, Mixtos and Mercancias. These are roughly equivalent to Express, consisting of passenger vehicles only, with a top speed of 50 km/hr (31.25 m.p.h.); Mail trains, with limited numbers of goods wagons, able to run at 45 km/hr (28.12 m.p.h.); Mixed trains, perhaps performing shunting duties en-route, with a running speed of 37 km/hr (23.12 m.p.h.), and Goods trains whose maximum permitted speed was a mere 30 km/hr (18.75 m.p.h.). When the railcars were introduced, those travelling alone were classed as Rápidos and timed at 60 km/hr (37.5 m.p.h.), while towing up to two trailers classed the train as a Ligero limited to 50 km/hr. (31.25 m.p.h.).

The extremely slow speed of the goods trains is a reminder that no continuous brake was fitted to freight vehicles. This was covered by an operating regulation stating that unfitted trains should contain one vehicle in six fitted with a screw-brake. The practice of running with a brake van at each end of the train must stem from this rule, and perhaps explains why some 1950s era pictures show brake vans marshalled in the middle of passenger rakes. (It is by no means certain that all the original four-wheeled carriages were vacuum fitted). As a number of the vans and wagons were fitted with a brake standard and an open-air seat for a brakeman it is possible that they were used to augment the brake vans when required. It must be said that a journey from Palma to Arta perched on one of the roof-top seats can hardly have been a pleasant experience! However the brakemen were not the only staff working outside the train. Travelling ticket inspectors formerly visited each coach while the train was in motion by walking along the running boards, providing the reason for the provision

The Palma station pilot, No 4, pauses while shunting at the terminus while produce is unloaded from the vans in the train, 2nd October 1957. (L.G. Marshall)

CAMPOS shunting an open wagon on the coaling road at Palma. 8th August 1962. (J.K. Williams)

of long horizontal hand-rails which were fitted to the four-wheeled carriages. This practice which was perhaps a hang-over from British methods dating back to the line's Victorian origins, was also common on at least one other Spanish narrow gauge line, the Santander-Bilbao Railway, where it lasted well into the 1950s.

Other operating regulations gave the maximum loads to be attached to the different types of locomotive, according to the route or the type of train; where a train was above the appropriate tonnage then extra time was allowed on the more steeply graded sections of the line, at a rate of 30 seconds per kilometre for each 10 tonnes of excess weight. In snowy or wet weather the loads had to be reduced to the next lower category. When double-heading was employed the train's tonnage was to be 90% of the total capability of the two engines. With goods trains comprising twenty to thirty loaded wagons in the railway's heyday, double heading was a not uncommon occurrence. Finally, wagons whose loads weighed more than 4 tonnes were not allowed to travel at more that 40 km/hr, thus regulating them to the mixed or goods services.

After the State take-over in 1951 the Arta and La Puebla services were each reduced to two daily trains for some years, although by 1954 the service frequency had been increased and the working pattern was quite complicated, and it is obvious that there were often quite substantial changes to the schedules from year to year. The steam-powered Correo had taken three and a half hours to reach Arta including a twenty-five minute stop at Manacor; while part of this time would have been spent taking on water, it seems that the section beyond Manacor was almost treated as a separate branch with an end-on connection. Passenger trains dropped carriages at Manacor before continuing on to Arta, and while this may be mainly due to the poorer traffic potential, the fact that the goods locomotives could not carry sufficient water to reach the far terminus meant that mixed trains were the rule on this section.

By 1959 the published timetable shows what an impact the new diesel railcars were making. Without the need to perform shunting duties, the new railcars cut the journey time between Palma and Arta to just two hours and eight minutes. Similarly the journey time of the first inward service from Manacor to Palma was cut from two hours and nine minutes to one hour thirty-five minutes. On all lines the last train on public holidays was held back to depart between one and two hours later than usual. In 1959 the railcars were generally based at the outer termini. The traffic pattern on the La Puebla branch was different with some of the services being locomotive hauled while others were worked by railcars. The Arta services, shared by steam and diesel, were even more complicated with some trains only working between Palma and Manacor. Lodging turns for the train crews were common and accommodation was available in the station at Arta, and also at Inca, Manacor, Felanitx and Santany as well as at Palma. At one time staff quarters were also in use at Empalme but this may have been for track-side workers, who were also catered for at Llubi.

Changes in the 1963 timetable included the substitution of a railcar on many of the erstwhile steam services, including the afternoon Palma-Arta Correo. This railcar now left the capital one hour later than the old steam departure time, but reached Arta only a few minutes later than the previous timing. The same railcar was then booked to return to Palma after a short wait at Arta. Two of the round trips between Arta and Palma are not marked AUTO (railcar) so may have been diesel-hauled, possibly providing mixed workings although the timings are as tight as the railcar schedules and would allow little or no time for shunting en-route. One B-B diesel would have been required for these services.

The Santany line experienced minor retimings as did the La Puebla branch which was now provided with four daily return services, worked by one railcar. The main beneficiaries of the new timetable were the users of the Felanitx branch who regained an extra railcar service in each direction thus helping to fill the service gaps in the morning and afternoon which had existed for some years. The first railcar from Palma now left at 09.25 instead of 14.15 as previously, with an extra departure from Felanitx at 12.30.

By 1965 a major change had occurred with the closure of the Santany branch. To compensate there were now several short trips between Palma and Inca which would have absorbed the Santany drivers, though their home shed would perforce have moved to Palma. Crew rosters on the lines to Felanitx and La Puebla would have been unaltered, but the working patterns on the Arta line could have been simplified with only the B-B diesel being based there to work the two daily runs to Palma.

No 52, one of the 2-6-2Ts, taking water at Manacor before leaving with the 5.12pm for Palma, 6th May 1958.
(D. Winkworth)

Krupp-built No 31 heading a Felanitx-Palma goods train pauses at Porreras, 10th June 1960.   (Mike Swift)

The year 1974 saw the end of goods services and with them the end for the need for locomotive-hauled trains. Although two of the B-B locomotives were retained for a time, they cannot have been much employed. The 1975 timetable shows the railcars making five daily round trips to both La Puebla and Arta, though it is possible that the Arta line returned to three trips before its eventual closure in 1977. The 1978 season included eighteen services linking Palma and Inca, with four of these continuing to La Puebla. By this time all crews were based at Palma, and timings had once again been cut. In 1960 the steam train timings between Palma and La Puebla had been almost two hours, with one hour fourteen minutes allowed for the railcars. By 1978 the latter timings had been cut by eight minutes to one hour and six minutes. Contemporary travellers tell of the railcars being taken up to the maximum allowed speed despite the fairly poor state of the track which gave a somewhat rough ride; This was certainly borne out by an examination of the track on the La Puebla branch shortly after its closure, which came in March 1981. Present services only run as far as Inca, although the track relaying and the use of continuous welded rail has once again helped to shorten the journey timings. Nowadays the maximum permitted speed, at least on straight sections of the line, is 120 km/hr (75 m.p.h)

The transitional years between steam and diesel power attracted the attention of a few enthusiasts and the following accounts of the contemporary scene are of interest. The first was written by the late Kenneth Hartley, who spent an afternoon on the railway in 1957 just before the widespread introduction of the new diesel railcars. The author is grateful to the Editor of THE NARROW GAUGE (the journal of the Narrow Gauge Society) for permission to include it here, as it paints a graphic picture of the line in the last days of steam.

"There were many unusual features to note, sketch or photograph, not to mention a very basic train service of three trains a day from Palma to anywhere except Inca - which was served by eight, including expresses - that one needed a week or so to cover the lines then in operation. However the steam railway was by no means the only attraction in Majorca, although it was the best. Hence, to see as many trains as possible in a limited time, I decided that Santa Maria was my best choice, as the double track main line ran through this junction en-route to Inca, as well as to La Puebla, Arta and Felanitx. In fact the only passenger trains not serving Santa Maria were those on the Santany branch, which left the main line soon after leaving Palma station. On 3rd July 1957 I got a 2nd return and travelled on the 12.30pm departure for Inca. This consisted of 2-6-0 tank number 9 with two of the superior bogie coaches numbers 111 and 112 and brake van F20. The guard saw that I was trying to get a shot of our train, and with customary Spanish courtesy held it back until I had got aboard. Soon after stopping at Pont d'Inca we passed De Dion railcar A3, and without stops at either Marratxi or a small halt further up the line arrived at the junction at 1.05pm, my intention being to catch the 2.55pm back to Palma. The first arrival was a 1.30pm from Inca; Krupp 2-6-0 tank 33 with four 1st and 2nd class four-wheelers and a brake at each end. A few minutes after this train left for Palma, No 21 SANTANY came in with a light load of three four wheelers and brake F1 - again for Palma.

There was then a pause until about 2.35pm so I went into the village in search of a cold drink, returning to the station in time to see No 30 arrive with a four-wheeler of each class - 1st, 2nd and 3rd. The whistle on this locomotive was deep toned, like the old Great Central Railway. As the train departed No 9 returned with its two bogies and brake and I was so intent on getting a shot of this, that I failed to note the time. Also almost before I had turned my film to the next exposure a most exciting train came into view, going "hell for leather" and bound for Manacor and Arta. It belted through the station at express speed, headed by 2-6-2 tank No 55 - the load was two or three bogies, five four-wheelers, six goods vans and a couple of brakes. It was quite a few minutes after this exhilarating sight before I realised that I'd missed my train to Palma - and that the next one was not until about 7.00pm.

It was a long wait, but by no means entirely wasted. I had another much needed ice-cold orangeade in the village; was shown the process of making various types of coloured tiles in a little works adjacent to the station; and initiated into the art of drinking, more or less successfully, from a Spanish drinking vessel. Also there were several interesting arrivals and departures, first of which was 2-6-2 tank No 51 with one bogie, six four-wheelers, six goods vans, a cattle truck and two brakes. By way of contrast the next arrival was the little 0-6-0 tank No 5 with a train of a dozen assorted goods wagons headed by a brake and tailed by one of those old 3rd/brake

Railcar A4 and Correo/2nd class coach at Felanitx on 10th June 1960. The train had left Palma at 14.15 and appears to have arrived ahead of the 15.46 timing according to the station clock.   (Mike Swift)

One of the B-B diesels pauses at Inca with a train bound for Arta.   (Mike Swift)

composites - the only time I ever saw one in use. This halted on the centre track, to allow railcar A3 - without trailers - to pull into the platform a few minutes later, pause briefly and then turn off onto the Felanitx branch. After this, No 5 had quite a busy time, rearranging her train, and inserting a waiting flat truck loaded with peaches. Finally, with a shrill whistle, she slowly moved off with her load, curving away down the line to Felanitx.

Hardly had No 5 got out of sight when No 15 ALARO brought in a 24-wagon goods train from Palma. The 4-6-0 spent some time in shunting various loaded and empty coal wagons, picked up a flat wagon loaded with barrels, and finally departed for Inca. About half an hour later a train for Palma arrived - earlier than I'd expected - and I was happy to join it. Krupp 2-6-0 No 30 was our motive power for the three coach train, and seemed to be running on a mere whiff of steam, as the gradients were mostly favourable - the fireman in fact travelled for much of the journey sitting on the edge of the footplate, hanging onto the cab handrails at arms length. We arrived in Palma at 7.00pm, a busy time with railcars A2 and A4 - this latter with two well filled trailers - in the station. 4-4-0 tank ARTA was shunting coaches, No 21 tank was on a train bound, I think, for Inca; and No 31 Krupp was in steam in the locomotive yard. A fitting end to a very satisfactory outing over a small part of the Majorcan Railways."

Another visitor to the island was K.P.Plant who made several journeys over the system in June 1960. By this time the change to diesel haulage was well under way, although steam power was still holding its own. After spending the morning of June 10th recording the locomotives in and around the sheds and workshops at Palma, K.P.P. caught the 2.15pm service to Felanitx. This was composed of railcar A-4 towing one of the Correo/2nd class carriages, number 34. The train left a few minutes late and arrived at Felanitx at 3.45pm. Here there were about eight wagons in the yard, plus the partially dismantled remains of No 11 ALGAIDA in the engine shed. At some stage of the afternoon another train must have arrived as by the time the railcar returned to Palma at 5.30pm, Krupp 2-6-0T number 31 had appeared and was making up a goods train of six wagons bracketed by a brake van at either end. The goods was supposed to follow the railcar back to Palma but apparently used to leave "when the Maquinista (driver) felt like it". K.P.P. hitched a lift in the front brake van in the company of the Jefe del Tren (the Trainmaster, responsible for the running of the train, the paperwork relating to the freight being carried, and who on a passenger service would work with a ticket inspector), and a youth who operated the brake wheel. Another brakeman rode in the tail-end van. Departure from Felanitx was delayed until 5.56pm, while about half an hour later the train was leaving Porreras, Montuiri being reached about ten minutes later at 6.37pm. Some smart shunting appears to have taken place as K.P.P's notes mention "very good traffic in small consignments and full wagons". Despite this the train was on its way again at 6.45pm and reached Algaida at 6.54pm. A visit to a nearby cafe for a drink with the crew ("not allowed to leave the train, really") seems to have delayed the departure until almost 7.07pm. Santa Eugenia was reached fourteen minutes later and here station work only took three minutes - possibly a small consignment being loaded into the front brake van. The main line junction at Santa Maria was reached at 7.34pm and the train rested until 7.54pm, probably to allow other traffic to clear the main line. There was no work to do at Marratxi which was passed without stopping, while a pause at Pont D'Inca added another two minutes to the journey. The train finally arrived back at Palma at 8.19pm. This was presumably the homeward leg of the daily Felanitx goods turn. Railcars left Palma at 7.30am 12.30pm and 5.30pm, arriving at Felanitx at 10.56am, 2.56pm and 8.56pm. so the outward goods probably followed the middle railcar working. This should have resulted in a mid-afternoon arrival at the outer terminus in plenty of time for a "booked" departure around 5.45pm - though this was obviously flexible.

The next day saw K.P.P. sample the service to La Puebla aboard the 9.00am departure from Palma. This train was made up of one of the new railcars, number 2001 and trailer number 5001. As well as the driver, the train crew included the Jefe del Tren and a Conductor, unlike the previous day's service which only carried a crew of two. Nevertheless there was room for K.P.P. to sit on the second seat beside the driver. At Inca a permanent way gang were busy with some welding work, and had arrived at the site aboard a yellow petrol trolley. Further on at Empalme the driver, "an apprentice of about forty" left the train and the Conductor took over the controls. Up to now speeds had been about 55 - 60km/hr, but the new man took the train up to 70km/hr, almost its maximum permitted speed, despite the somewhat indifferent state of the track. After Llubi the line had been reballasted and the riding was easier. An ancient blue bus belonging to the railway company met the train at Muro, presumably a service to the outlying villages. For the last couple of miles the line passed through fields of beans and potatoes watered by what seemed like hundreds of windmills. These were set on a base of stone blocks and had large ten-sided vaned wheels with a large arrow-shaped tail to keep them facing the wind; a few of these are still left in the island today. Refreshment was available on this journey as the railcar's luggage area carried a supply of crated beer and soft drinks selling at 5 pesetas a bottle.

The terminus at La Puebla was reached at 10.15am and there was time to note the old double engine shed, though one track had been lifted. Meanwhile the railcar ran round its trailer and made ready to leave. Departure was at 12.35pm (five minutes late) with a 1.05pm arrival at Inca where K.P.P. left the train to await the connecting service to Manacor. This arrived shortly afterwards and was formed of B-B diesel 1101 hauling four bogie carriages and a brake van. This train left Inca at 1.27pm and ran non-stop to Sineu with K.P.P. aboard the rear coach, a 1st/2nd composite. Along the way the train's progress was watched by crossing keepers who carried a stick with red and green flags at opposite ends. Sineu station saw a large exodus from the train, and at Petra a 16-seater bus marked Petra - Ariany was seen in the station yard. Speeds between stations were fast on this section and the well sprung coach bounced its occupants around, there being no arm-rests between the seats. Manacor was reached at 2.12pm.

K.P.P. left the train (which possibly terminated here) and explored the surroundings. A Nasmyth 4-6-0T Number 12 SAN JUAN was discovered in the locomotive shed in good condition along with the derelict chassis of railcar A-1. In another shed were two Maquinista-built 2-6-0Ts, both derelict and rusty and with all identification removed, though one had 7 chalked on it. In the station yard was a 25-seater bus bound for the resort of Porto Cristo. Built by General Motors it was owned by a private bus operator.

Later 2-6-2T number 53 arrived with a train of a brake van, five bogie coaches and five vans. After much shunting the train was whittled down to the brake, two coaches and eight assorted goods wagons, and although due to leave for Arta at 4.23pm all this activity delayed the departure until 4.40pm. Further up the line a wagon of timber was dropped off at San Lorenzo, and there was time to take some photographs during a pause at Son Servera. Arta was finally reached at 5.43pm (due 5.20pm). Rapid shunting soon disposed of the wagons, while two more bogie coaches were picked up to strengthen the return working. Nevertheless the train managed to depart at 5.56pm, only six minutes behind schedule. Back at Manacor another bogie carriage was added to the train which left at 6.47pm, overtaking a Palma-bound goods, headed by B-B diesel number 1102 at Petra. The passenger train arrived at Palma at 8.21pm, having taken two hours and twenty five minutes for the journey.

At Palma 0-6-0T number 5, seen complete the previous day, had now had its tanks removed, and the underframe of railcar A-3 was also noted - the body apparently in the Carpenters' Shop undergoing repairs.

The following day was taken up by a trip on the Santany line. The train was again composed of railcar number 2001 and trailer number 5001, and left Palma "packed to the boards" a few minutes after the scheduled time of 9.20am. At Coll d'en Rabassa there was a cheese factory next to the line and a military airfield (the present commercial airport) was visible on the left hand side. Arenal saw a massive disembarkation, but despite this the train only managed to reach 45 km/hr when climbing the gradient out of the station. Second gear was needed on this stretch. The summit was reached at kilometre 24 and by this time fields had replaced the scrub and woodland that had persisted since Arenal. After Lluchmayor a long straight allowed the speed to reach 75 km/hr on a well-maintained length where the railcar rode well. From Lluchmayor to Campos the line was on a falling gradient while beyond Campos was another straight stretch through the fields.

Santany was reached at 10.50am. In the shed was a partly dismantled and anonymous 4-6-0T, thought to be number 13, LLOSETA. The rest of the station was picturesque, with a very attractive garden surrounding the well. There appeared to be little goods activity, as by this time the branch freight train only ran three times a week, on Mondays, Thursdays and Saturdays, leaving Palma at 9.30am and returning when ready. The railcar left Santany at 12.45pm for the return to Palma. The 9 kilometre long climb from Campos to Lluchmayor was a steady grind in second gear at speeds of 45 - 50 km/hr. One motor got extremely hot under this treatment, the temperature gauge showing 85 degrees, with 90 marked DANGER. The second motor remained at 75 degrees although the paintwork on both was blistered. (The Bussing motors often gave trouble and several railcars suffered fires; later, Pegaso engines were fitted to overcome this problem.) At intermediate stations flagmen were in attendance on the loop points, as trains were not allowed to enter a station until signalled by flag or lamp. Incidentially, flag signals followed former British practice, with Red for Danger, Green for Caution, and White for All Clear. At Lluchmayor three more anonymous locomotives were found in the engine shed; two were 4-4-0Ts (thought to be numbers 22 SALINAS and 27 ARTA) while the other was a Maquinista 2-6-0T (possibly number 9) which was lacking its centre wheels. Back aboard the railcar speeds of 80 km/hr was achieved coasting down the long slope to Arenal, and the arrival back at Palma was made at 2.11pm.

Before leaving the subject of train working the discovery of the Freight Consignment book for Llubi station plus a few scattered recollections of visitors to the railway before 1974 allow one or two comments to be made concerning goods workings on the system. Important stations were provided with a Stationmaster, a Goods Clerk and two Porters. Small stations had to get by with only the Stationmaster and one Porter to cover all the duties including some considerable paperwork.

At Llubi almost all the outgoing goods wagons were filled with small mixed consignments. The main exception was a van that carried milk to Palma every day. This was such a regular traffic that during the summer of 1939 van number C208 was habitually thus employed. Although the milk was usually the only load for this vehicle, a large number of consignments on 29th July that year resulted in the unlikely combination of milk and soap being carried to Palma in the same van; hopefully the two consignments were kept well apart! On the same day open wagon number B121 was sent away loaded to Pont D'Inca but also carrying apricots for Manacor. Presumably one of these consignments was off-loaded en-route while the train waited. Open wagon number A10 was dispatched to Palma with not only several assorted consignments of mixed fruit, but also potatoes for Santa Maria, apricots for Porreras and fruit for Arenal. Loads travelling up the branch to La Puebla are rare and when they occur a wagon number is rarely given. This is probably because the items travelled in the brake van, or were loaded into a wagon with spare room, but whose number was unknown until the train's arrival.

A special check was kept on consignments of alcohol in any form, which were obviously entered up in a separate book as their docket numbers are included in the Freight Consignment register. As well as fruit and vegetables, Llubi's main exports were soap, milk, liquor and eggs - all usually travelling in C-class vans, but also occasionally dispatched in open wagons. Livestock was also dealt with on a regular basis; horses, pigs, goats and calves were commonly carried, while on 22nd December 1939 eighty-eight turkeys were sent to Palma! Other loadings that have been observed are class A open wagons containing coal, B-class opens carrying bundles of firewood, stone building blocks or manure, the latter being sent out to the country stations from the stables of Palma for use as fertilizer. Carboys of olive oil, large wine barrels or fruit in baskets were also handled in B-class wagons, which were also used for ballast or sleepers when the Vias Y Obras needed a train to help with track renewals.

Goods traffic on the Alaró tramway had always been handled in FC de Mallorca wagons, and these also ran through to Soller, despite the differing couplings on the two railways. At least one FC de M van was provided with a Soller-style screw coupling in addition to its "chopper" and it may be that this was used as a converter wagon - otherwise staff may have trusted to merely hooking the safety chains together.

Freight traffic charges were divided into two categories:- Gran Velocidad and Pequeña Velocidad, (roughly equivalent to Fast traffic - by passenger/mixed train, and Slow traffic - by goods train) with the rates set according to the speed of delivery. The Gran Velocidad service appears to have been suspended in 1964 in line with the policy of replacing all passenger services with the new railcars which were unsuitable for hauling a tail load of goods vehicles. In any case G.V. receipts had declined over the previous ten years from 340,000 pesetas in 1955 to 81,000 pesetas in 1962, with a sharp drop in 1959. The receipts from Pequeña Velocidad traffic was seven times that of the faster service in 1955, and by 1963 receipts had reached a total of 2,250,000 pesetas. That same year the faster service managed a slight revival to 114,000 pesetas, but this was not enough to prevent its withdrawal. The trend seems to have been of a slow decline in goods traffic, as the next year goods receipts only amounted to 1,944,000 pesetas. The reasons for this are probably twofold:- those shippers who needed a guaranteed speedy service would have had to turn to road haulage, while the railway - now that steam power had been laid aside - had less potential motive power available for a full range of goods and mixed trains, while the latter were gradually disappearing from the timetable. The trains not designated as Auto (railcars) would still have been locomotive hauled and able to convey goods wagons, while the four B-B diesels would in theory have been enough to cover the four routes. However by this time all services to Felanitx and Santany were by railcar, and with dwindling goods traffic freight services may have been worked on an "as required" basis, hardly justifying the retention of four locomotives. It is thus hardly surprising that two of the four diesels were returned to the mainland around 1968, the others following shortly afterwards.

As goods working diminished during the 1960s wagons were laid aside and slowly scrapped, although a large number were left at Palma for some years afterwards. Apart from the van already noted on the FC de Soller at least one other FC de Mallorca vehicle followed it to the neighbouring line. This was open wagon number B132 which has been converted into a weed-killing tank wagon and can usually be seen stored in a siding at Soller.

The FC de Soller's station at Palma in 1957. Nearest to the camera is a van from the FC de Mallorca which appears to have an adapted coupling for use with Soller rolling stock.   (L.G. Marshall)

PART TWO: THE SOLLER RAILWAY AND TRAMWAY

Chapter 7
A History of the Soller Railway

Although a road, climbing over the Sierra de Alfabia to link Palma and the north coast, had been opened in the 1840s, it was clear by the end of the century that a more rapid means of communication was essential to serve Soller. In 1892 a proposal was drawn up for a railway linking the town with Palma running west of the mountains via Valldemosa, Esporles and Son Sardina, however the cost of this circuitous route was too great to be economically viable, and the scheme lapsed. In 1903 the Town Council of Soller again discussed the possibility of a rail link by tunnelling through the mountains; this time the plan failed as it was felt that the technical difficulties of such an undertaking were too great. However the latter idea was revived a year later and an engineer, Pedro Garau, was appointed to draw up plans for the line including a tunnel 2.8 kilometres long at the summit of the railway. The total length of the proposed line was twenty seven kilometres.

On 31st July 1905 the Compañia Ferrocarril de Soller S.A. (Soller Railway Company Ltd.) was formed to build the line, with a capital of £131,500 divided into 7,000 shares. Such was the enthusiasm for the proposed rail link that the entire share issue was subscribed by local inhabitants within a couple of days. The scope of the plan was enlarged slightly in 1908 to include an extension to Puerto de Soller. As originally conceived the railway's length would have failed to attract a Government subsidy that was available to the builders of lines of thirty kilometres or more. However, despite the subsidy, more money had to be raised for the extension and the total amount of share capital was increased to £163,000, though later it had to be augmented yet again to a total of £208,700. This worked out at £6,732 per kilometre, mostly accounted for by the expenses of tunnelling. A gauge of 3 feet was proposed to match the island's existing railway system and also to reduce costs. Steam haulage was planned between Palma and Soller, while the extension was to be built as an electric tramway.

The construction of the railway was undertaken by Luís Borio who undertook to complete the trackbed in thirty four months, work starting in June 1907, though eventually tunnelling difficulties extended the construction period until August 1910. In all, thirteen tunnels were required plus a long viaduct and a number of bridges to bring the line through the mountains. At the northern end of the main tunnel the line was at an altitude of 210 metres above sea level, while the station at Soller was set at only 40 metres; thus the railway was obliged to descend in a series of loops almost amounting to a spiral for the last nine kilometres into Soller. Even so, the ruling gradient of this section is a challenging 1 in 45.

Tracklaying began at Palma in April 1911, and the contractor acquired a small four-coupled engine which had previously worked on the Palma Tramways. Named "MARIA LUISA" on its arrival on the Soller line, it had been built by the Falcon Works of Loughborough, England, in about 1891. Once tracklaying started the work proceeded speedily, the original sleepers being pine or oak, spaced at 600 per kilometre. The permitted axle-load was 9 tons. The rails reached the northern end of the Alfabia tunnel towards the end of July 1911, and on July 25th a special train carrying the Directors, shareholders and various dignitaries was run to the new railhead. Construction trains began running to Soller on 19th August, attracting great crowds, and the following year, on 16th April 1912, the line was officially opened, although goods trains had been running for the previous month.

The company had taken delivery of three 2-6-0 tank locomotives built by La Maquinista, two of which double-headed the inaugural train over the line. Shortly afterwards another similar locomotive was obtained and the Falcon tram locomotive was taken into the company's stock. To cater for passenger traffic ten bogie carriages were obtained from Carde y Escoriaza, together with twenty four assorted goods wagons built by Orenstein & Koppel.

Having opened the railway to Soller, the Directors considered a possible extension westwards from Palma, into an area as yet untapped by existing railways. The town of Andratx was a likely goal, but the scheme

77

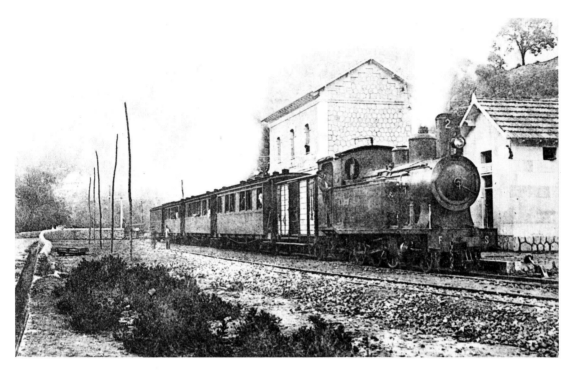

A train bound for Palma pauses at Bunyola shortly after the opening of the FC de Soller.   (J. Wiseman)

28 – SÒLLER. Detalle de la línea del ferrocarril

An early view of a steam train nearing Soller.   (J.K. Williams collection)

never progressed further than the planning stage. Presumably the area was adequately served by the existing roads or by sea via Puerto Andratx.

The tramway extension to Puerto de Soller was completed in September 1913 and services started on 4th October that year. At first they were run with three tramcars and two trailers, but later more vehicles were added to the fleet. A small power-station was established at Soller, the tramcars' traction motors picking up the 600v dc current via bow collectors from the overhead cable. There are indications that a through service from Palma to Puerto de Soller may have been planned in the early days, as a photograph shows a train of railway stock at the port in 1929, but this practice was not in fact continued.

The railway company had under-estimated the line's traffic potential and it was not long before extra goods wagons had to be obtained bringing their total up to thirty eight. However this success also brought problems as it was found that the locomotives were somewhat underpowered. The almost continuous up-grades for some half the journey in either direction limited potential loads, without double-heading, to something under 100 tonnes and added to this was the inconvenience of having to stop to take on water en-route. This double-heading made a nonsense of the economics of running the line and no doubt the engines were driven hard in an effort to offset their shortcomings. Because of this maintainance costs were soon higher than had been anticipated and the company began to operate at a deficit. Steam power was proving something of a liability, and by the mid 1920s it was clear that a major change was needed.

The railway company sought the advice of German experts who suggested a plan to electrify the whole line at a cost of £73,600. This was agreed in July 1926, but it was not until three years later on July 14th 1929 that the new services commenced. The electrified services were provided by four bogie saloon motor coaches, which hauled trains made up of the original carriages. At the same time four new carriages were added to the company's stock list, with three bogie brake/luggage vans arriving shortly afterwards.

Electricity for the trains was obtained from the island's power station at Palma, via a substation at Bunyola which supplied the 1200V dc traction current through Mercury-arc rectifiers. However there were initial teething troubles and steam power was retained on some services until November 1929, after which the five locomotives were laid aside at Palma until 1944 when three were transferred to the FC de Mallorca.

The development of tourism in the 1950s brought an upsurge in passenger traffic as visitors discovered the magnificent scenery through which the line passed. In 1955 the railway carried 331,000 passengers and the tramway 800,000 and by 1960 this had risen to 421,570 railway and 861,194 tramway passengers. The same year 17,000 tons of goods were carried. Assuming that freight was only carried on six days of the week, this is a daily average of 54.5 tons or perhaps half a dozen wagon loads. During the following decade the passenger figures increased, though the Tramway's returns declined slightly between 1967 and 1970. In 1971 the number of railway travellers had increased to almost 575,000.

While the railway's power was now obtained from the national grid via Palma there were nevertheless occasional problems with the overhead power supply, which was vulnerable to lightning strikes, resulting in train services being suspended during thunderstorms. To overcome this the railway bought a diesel in 1968 to act as stand-by motive power. D-1 is a 29 ton B-B locomotive, built in Germany and imported through Ferrotrade. It is fitted with a 500hp engine with Voith transmission that delivers 470 hp at 200 rpm, and is capable of maintaining services with a five coach train.

The railway's passsenger traffic continued to increase until 1975, though some economies were made, notably the withdrawal of goods services in 1972. However despite the railway's passenger success, the number of Tramway passengers continued to decline, only relieved by an upturn for a couple of years early in the 1980s. In 1983 719,193 passengers were carried and this figure marked a peak on the Tramway for a while; that same year the railway carried 754,590 travellers. For the rest of the mid 1980s the Tramway continued its decline, perhaps due in part to increasing local car ownership.

A Government report by INECO on the island's transport systems provides a useful "snapshot" of the FC de Soller at the beginning of the 1980s. Installations and maintenance facilities, as well as rolling stock, were

Motor coach No 2 waits for the "off" at Palma in 1960.   (Michael Andress)

A visit to Bunyola in 1984 revealed this special train - diesel D1 is seen propelling one of the brake vans towards Palma in the wake of a scheduled passenger train.   (Author)

described as obsolete - although it was admitted that the antique motive power was one of the reasons why the line was popular with tourists. Ordinary fares were 3.20 pesetas/km for 1st Class, 2.50 pesetas/km for 2nd Class - higher than either the FEVE line or even the national average, but given the special nature of the line they were not considered unreasonable. Workers, students and season ticket holders paid half the normal fare, while a special return rate of 160 pesetas applied to the daily "Tourist Special" departure from Palma. In general track maintenance was being carried out with 1000 - 1500 sleepers being replaced each year. New rail was needed in places, but it appeared that none of a suitable weight (35km/metre) was currently available.

The report recommended work to improve safety on the urban section of the line in Palma, the urgent relaying of the Palma to Bunyola section with 45kg/metre rail - to be completed as soon as possible, as well as immediate renovation work on two of the longest tunnels. The workshops also needed to be brought up to date as a matter of urgency, and a five year plan was suggested to modernise the rolling stock. Finally, the railway's telephone system needed to be upgraded immediately.

A policy of catering more and more to the tourist industry was established, and visitors have been encouraged to visit Soller by railway, a daily "Tourist Special" departing from Palma at 10.40am. All this succeeded in raising passenger numbers to 758,467 by 1987, when the Company's official returns showed an operating profit of 6.2 million pesteas and dividends were once more being paid to the shareholders. Improvements have been made to the trackwork and bridges as recommended and the line now seems to have an assured future.

A mixed train leaving Palma on 21st February 1955 comprises motor coach No 3, one carriage and a brake van, with two vans and three open wagons bringing up the rear.   (Brian Butt)

Motor coach No 2 shunting at Palma in January 1988. (Author)

FS Saloon carriage. (L.G. Marshall)

Chapter 8
Locomotives and Rolling Stock

The Steam Locomotives

Little can now be traced of the tram locomotive MARIA LUISA, however by comparing various details that can be discerned in surviving photographs, the engine appears to have been the type produced by Falcon for the heaviest type of tramway work. This type, details of which are given on page 19 of the firm's 1889 Illustrated Catalogue of Locomotive Engines, was supplied for lines of 3 ft gauge and upwards and came in three different power classes depending on the chosen cylinder size. Cylinders measuring 9 by 14 inches, 10 by 14 inches and 10.5 by 14 inches were available, but unfortunately details of which were fitted to MARIA LUISA are no longer available. Falcon sources suspect that the engine may have been a hybrid with features belonging to different types of the "standard" tram engines.

Returning to the "standard" dimensions, it is likely that the Majorcan engine had a wheelbase measuring 5 ft and wheels 2 ft 6.5 inches in diameter. The catalogue views are almost broadside, so an albeit rough and ready estimation gives a probable overall length (excluding buffers) of 13 ft 6 inches. However, it must be stressed that these dimensions are something in the nature of speculation.

The engine had an almost totally enclosed body constructed of metal, resembling a normal passenger tramcar, but without the end platforms. The buffer beam extended downwards to track level and at one time metal skirts covered the wheels and motion which employed a system, named after its inventor Charles Brown, where the locomotive's cylinders were mounted above the footplate and the drive to the rear wheels was by means of a rocker arm. A simple stove-pipe chimney emerged above the arc roof which in the early days was devoid of other equipment. By the locomotive's retirement photographs show that a large but indistict "lump" had been added to the roof, possibly condensing gear.

The four locomotives supplied by La Maquinista have already been covered in the section dealing with the FC de Mallorca. While employed on the FC de Soller they carried the following names and numbers:- No. 1 SOLLER, No. 2 PALMA, and No. 3 BUNYOLA (all completed by 3rd March 1912) and No. 4 SON SARDINA (completed on 15th September 1912). Numbers 1 - 3 eventually passed to the FC de Mallorca, while No. 4 and the tram locomotive were scrapped in 1944. While running on the Soller line they carried large Continental style brass locomotive lamps on the front buffer beam though these do not seem to have survived the move to the neighbouring system, where a less flamboyant British pattern of lamp was carried.

Internal Combustion Vehicles

The FC de Soller owns two other unusual items of rolling stock, both being rail conversions of contemporary road vehicles dating from the 1920s. The first is a 15hp Hispano Suiza lorry mounted on a short wheelbase railway chassis. Behind a conventional lorry bonnet and cab, the rest of the body resembles a large wooden box with small tool cabinets slung outboard on either side, pannier fashion. The box body supports a telescopic platform which is used for maintenance access to the overhead power wires. It is reported that the engine used the same set of spark plugs between the 1930s and the mid-1960s, though the fact that the vehicle has a very high petrol consumption (15 litres/3 gallons to make a one-way trip over the line) may have had something to do with this. In consequence it is infrequently used.

The other inspection car was built to overcome the fuel consumption of its companion, and uses only 4 litres of fuel per trip. It was produced in the Soller workshops by mounting a 1920s-era Renault car on railway axles having small disc wheels. The rest of the body is somewhat primitive and box-like having two doors, though these only extend to waist height and are open above. The motor is an 8hp Adler with four gears (three forward, one reverse). Both these vehicles are painted green.

The Motor-Coaches

With the electrification of the railway four motor-coaches were built by Carde y Escoriaza (numbers 1 - 4) and all are still in use today, each in turn being withdrawn for a year for a thorough overhaul. The bodies of these vehicles measure 14.35 metres and they are mounted on Brill type bogies constructed by the French firm

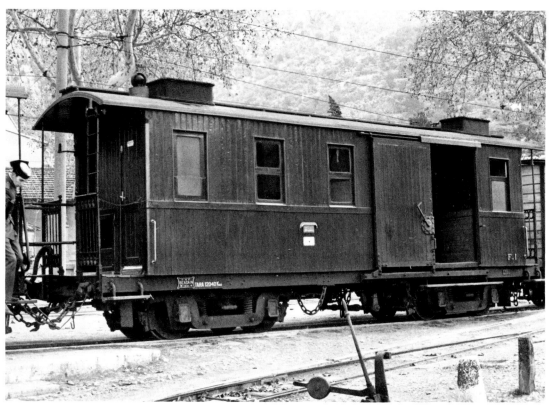

Brake van F1 at Soller.   (J-L Rochais, courtesy of J. Wiseman)

Palma goods yard showing the former high-sided open wagons. the cramped nature of the site can be appreciated.
(Michael Andress)

of Gallardon, and powered by two Siemens 120hp motors. The latter firm also supplied the pantographs, both of which are used in the raised position when running. The control gear was supplied by Schuckert. With a total load of 120 tonnes a top speed of 45 km/hr can be achieved on the line's ruling gradient; maximum permitted speed elsewhere is 50 km/hr. The total weight of the motor-coaches is 35 tonnes.

Behind the driving compartments at each end is an open sided platform providing passenger access. The driving compartments are set off-centre to allow the unused trailing compartment to be shut off; access to the rest of the train is then possible via the central doorway in the carriage end, and by fall-plates above the buffer/couplings.

All four motor-coaches offer both First and Second Class accommodation in separate compartments. First Class has twelve padded leather seats and in the case of No. 1 the original leather armchairs and settees have been retained. The Second Class compartments seat 32 passengers on slatted wooden seats. Externally the carriage bodies are finished in varnished teak.

The Carriage Stock.

Ten bogie saloon coaches were provided for the opening of the line cosisting of three First Class, four Composites and three Second Class vehicles. They had end balconies with decorative wrought iron handrails somewhat similar to those in use today. However the main difference was the provision of oil lighting with large lamp pots visible on the roof, which itself had an extra layer to ward off the heat of the sun.

Today's carriages total fourteen in number, six of which are of a slightly older pattern built by Carde y Escoriaza. The others are recent rebuilds or refurbishments carried out by the FC de Soller's workshops. These are characterised by having square windows with metal frames having rounded corners, and have been given bus-style seats. Length is 13.10 metres and the carriages weigh about 12,500 kilos though there are slight variations between individual vehicles. In 1984 the older pattern coaches were numbered 1 (the only remaining First Class saloon), 2 to 5 and 8, while the newer carriages were numbered 7 and 10 to 15. Number 9 seemed to be missing but may have been undergoing a rebuild at the time of the writer's visit. Carriage livery is varnished brown with black ironwork on the balconies. The running numbers are shown by small individual metal numbers, in similar style to the motor-coaches.

Brake Vans

For the opening of the line two brake vans were ordered from Carde y Escoriaza, but as the firm were unable to complete the vehicles in time they suggested the company should approach CAF Beasain who supplied two four-wheeled brake vans. However as even these failed to arrive in time the company were forced to begin operations using ordinary goods vans instead of brakes. The CAF vans were distinguished by having two shuttered ventilator panels high upon either side of a large central sliding door, with a long footboard between the axle-boxes. By 1929 their shortcomings must have become apparent; for one thing there could be no access for the train staff from the van to the rest of the train while it was in motion, so it was not surprising to find the company ordering some new brake vans. A van very similar to the original brake vans survived to the end of goods services, so the old brake vehicles may have been demoted to freight carriers in their later life. When this happened the footboards were removed. This would explain why in later years there were two styles of goods vans in evidence.

For the electrification CAF supplied some new bogie vans numbered F1 to F3. F1 and F2 arrived straight away, while the maker's plate on F3 is dated 1931. As well as providing an office desk for the Trainmaster's paperwork there was also plenty of room for parcels and luggage with a large sliding door on each side of the vehicle to facilitate loading. There was also a small postal compartment which boasted an exterior letter box in which letters could be placed for delivery at the train's destination. Like the carriages the new vans had end balconies, though their ironwork was of a slightly simpler pattern - a length of chain providing protection above the fall-plate, rather than the small gates with which the carriages were provided. The other new feature was the w.c. at each end of the van. In addition there was a dog-box opening off the balcony at one end.

Unlike the carriages, the vans' end balconies have the distinction of being lit by electric light, and a ladder is incorporated into the end railing, allowing access to the water tanks on the roof which supply the w.cs. As the vans always run at the Palma end of the train lamp brackets are only fitted to one end of the vehicle, however lamps are not carried in service. Van F1 alone has gained a window in its 'offside' sliding door.

Goods Stock

For the opening of the line two dozen wagons were provided by Orenstein & Koppel (Madrid), but this number was later increased to thirty eight vehicles by some wagons from Construcciones Metálicas de Llobregat. These carried a load of 10 tonnes compared with the 7 tonnes of the O & K vehicles. The final total consisted of 9 low-sided wagons (tare 3.4 tonnes), 16 high-sided open wagons (tare 4.1 tonnes) and 13 vans (tare 4.4 tonnes). There was also originally a crane mounted on bogies, though latterly a four-wheeled crane seems to

Two different FS van styles. The paler one is the type that was used as a temporary brake van in the lines earliest days.
(Michael Andress)

Close-up view of the railway/tramway coupling adapter. (Author)

have been in use. Almost the entire wagon fleet survived until at least 1974 when there were still all the vans and 20 other wagons still in existance. Now only a handfull of the low-sided wagons remain in service, together with one of the vans.

The original type of open wagon is typified by numbers B1 to B3 and number 4 which are one-plank dropside vehicles. B1 still retains a vertical screw brake handle while the others have conventional brake levers. Wagon B9, which is a one-plank wagon with fixed sides, appears to be one of the later wagons and has a heavier appearance with disc wheels rather than the open spokes of the other wagons. By 1988 wagons B2 and B9 had been fitted with 500 kg hoists to assist with tracklaying duties. These hoists are topped with an electric lamp, though there was no sign of a generator fitted to either wagon.

The last of the larger open wagons seems to have scrapped at some time after 1981 when it was seen loaded with scrap iron at Soller; by 1984 it had vanished. The body had five rather wide horizontal planks with central 'cupboard-style' doors and the axleboxes seemed to be similar to wagon B1.

Only one van, number 8, survived latterly though from its condition in 1984 it did not appear to have been used for some time, and may now have been scrapped. The body was interesting as the planks were of two alternating sizes and the panels on either side of the central doorways were not similar. There was a ventilation hatch at the top left hand corner of each side.

Goods wagon livery, if surviving at all, is a medium grey with all the ironwork picked out in black. The surviving wagons are all still fitted with continuous brake pipes as well as manual brakes. In service the wagons ran at the tail end of the train, behind the brake van on trains bound for Soller. Side chains as well as centre couplings were used. On the Soller wagons there was a screw coupling mounted below a large rectangular buffer rather than the "chopper" type used by the FC de Mallorca. "Foreign" wagons running through to Soller presumably merely relied on the safety chains being hooked up, although at least one FC de Mallorca van was fitted with a Soller-type screw coupling.

A weed-killing wagon has been converted from FC de Mallorca wagon B132, though little of the original body has lasted except for the metal strapping, and even part of the wagon's floor is missing. A large rectangular tank has been fitted, and a small petrol motor at one end drives a spray which discharges through a transverse pipe below the buffer beam. The wagon retains its vertical screw brake and FC de Mallorca couplings. These have been modified by removing the original hook and substituting a link to which is attached a Soller-type coupling loop, without the adjustable screw.

Apart from this service vehicle there are usually several trollies of assorted styles to be seen around the yard at Soller or at Bunyola, at one time including a partly completed railmotor in the process of being converted from a flat trolley.

The Trams

If you listen to the guides on the tourist excursion coaches that visit Puerto de Soller in the summer months, you will be told that the trams serving the resort date back to the turn of the century and that they were imported from San Francisco. This is a romantic story, but has little basis in reality. The fact is when the Tramway opened in 1913 three four-wheeled tramcars were supplied by the same combination of firms who eventually produced the railway's electric rolling stock:- Carde y Escoriaza (bodywork), Siemens-Schuckert (electrical equipment) and Brill (running gear), and it is these three cars, plus some later additions that provide the tram service today. The traction motors motors are rated at 35hp and air brakes are fitted, worked by a compressor. Electric current is picked up by a bow collector, though tram number 1 has been fitted with a railway-style pantograph to enable it to work as station pilot at Soller. In the 1950s this duty was carried out by number 3, which has now reverted to having a bow collector. As the trams employ a link and pin coupler, a coupling adaptor has to be temporarily attached so as to hook up to the railway stock. The older trams have varnished wooden bodies of narrow vertical teak planks, although the lower panels of the driving compartments are covered with metal sheeting, painted a bright orange colour. An all orange livery is also carried by the line's metal-bodied tramcar and its trailer. The trams' official capacity is 18 seated passengers, but in summer this number is augmented by as many standing passengers as can cram themselves aboard.

Two closed wooden trailers numbered 5 and 6 were also obtained in 1913. At about the same time four open 'toast-rack' trailers were purchased from the Palma Tramways for use in summer, and these were numbered 8 to 11. They date back to about 1890 and had originally been supplied by Carde y Escoriaza. They were designed to carry 24 passengers on transverse bench seats, though this number was later diminished when they were rebuilt with a central gangway and a gap in the end balcony at one end, to allow the Soller conductor access to collect fares. The open trailers thus run in permanently coupled pairs.

In 1959 another tramcar was obtained which was given the number 4. Basically similar in dimensions this car had the distinction of an all metal body and was purchased from the Bilbao Tramways along with another car which was converted into a closed trailer, number 7. Originally it had been intended to use both as power-cars, but however as the Bilbao Tramways were built to a wider gauge than the Soller system, certain problems were encountered in re-gauging the geared power trucks, and so the second car emerged from the works as a trailer.

The final vehicle which is sometimes seen on the tramway is a small cube-shaped refrigerated goods van used for fish traffic. This has a very short wheelbase and is painted in two shades of blue. It can occasionally be seen making the trip to and from the port attached to the rear of the tram trailers. In former days this duty was carried out by a small open truck, which may have provided the chassis for the refrigerated van.

During the line's freight carrying period goods wagons carried coal and other consignments through to the port. At one time the dockside layout contained a loop line, the site of which is now located within the Naval Base, and any necessary shunting here was carried out by a steam crane.

Tram No 3 has just run round its trailers at Soller and will shortly leave on the downhill run to the port, 11th July 1977. (K. Taylorson)

Chapter 9
The Soller Line Described

The Palma terminus of the FC de Soller is situated in the Plaza España next to the FEVE station, however the Soller station is much more attractive than its neighbour, the entrance archway with its decoratve lettering being shaded by a tall palm tree. The whole site is narrow and constricted, and there is just room for a single platform with a pleasant station bulding of brick faced with stone. The running line splits into three loops opposite the station, and there was formerly a line leading to a locomotive turntable and a three-stall semi-roundhouse. Today the stub end of this line terminates in a small wagon turntable used to turn the Permanent Way Department's motorised vehicles. Beside the station is a two-road brick shed which used to house the line's motor-coaches, and which these days occasionally shelters spare carriages. There was formerly a goods shed and a couple of short sidings for freight traffic at the outer end of the yard, all reached by a trailing siding and several wagon turntables. These too have now gone and today the site is a car park.

At the end of the station yard is a colour light signal, and beyond this the single line passes out through a gateway into the street where it runs along a central reservation flanked by low bushes. Several side streets cross the line in the first few hundred yards, and the train's whistle is in fairly constant use along this section of the line.

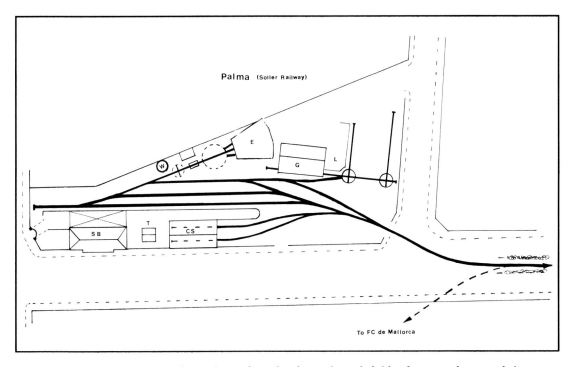

Leaving the city outskirts the track is unfenced and runs through fields of crops and scattered olive trees. Five kilometres after leaving the terminus the station of Son Sardina is reached. Here there is a single platform on the left of the line, and a small single-storey station building sheltered by trees. The loop track has an extra cross-over part of the way along it, plus a short dead-end siding. The gradient steepens slightly as the line runs on through the fields and after a further six kilometres the climb stiffens again to 1 in 50. There are a couple of 'request stop' halts in quick succession, merely short platforms with a simple shelter where the line crosses minor roads; the first and smaller halt is Santa Maria, while the other is named San Caubet and serves a nearby sanatorium. Across the road from this halt there was formerly an enclosed site that once had its own siding, though this has now been lifted and the buildings inside the enclosure are now derelict and partly demolished.

A quiet moment at Palma station in 1955.   (Brian Butt)

Son Sardina station looking towards Soller.   (Author)

Palma bound train at Bunyola on 25th October 1977. On the left is the line's inspection car.
(J-L Rochais, courtesy of J. Wiseman)

Bunyola station and goods shed looking towards Soller. (Author)

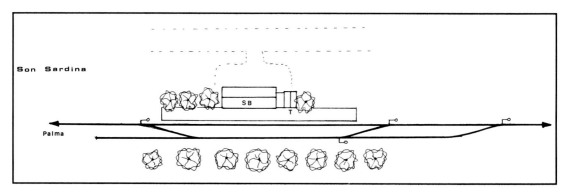

Son Sardina

Palma

Soon after this the climb flattens out and the train arrives at Bunyola, the mid-point crossing station on the railway. The station yard is most attractively situated on the edge of the town and is flanked by a row of pine trees. Approaching the station, the train passes the small electrical sub-station where the 15,000 volt power supply is converted to the railway's traction current of 1,200 volts d.c. Just after this the station loop opens up on the left, while on the right there is a trailing siding leading to a wagon turntable providing access to the modest goods shed which is nowadays used as a store by the Permanent Way Department. The passenger station is on the right hand side and the large clock overhanging the platform is worthy of note as it is shaped like an oversized pocket-watch. Besides the main platform there is also a shorter island platform between the tracks of the loop. As with the other stations on the line the turnouts are marked by point indicators, picked out in red and white paint.

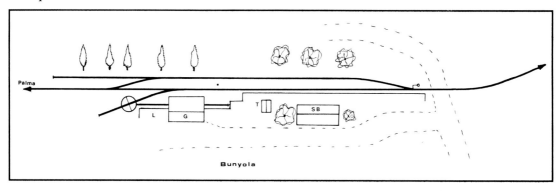

Palma

Bunyola

As the train leaves Bunyola it passes over another ungated level crossing and curves to the left. Ahead are steep hillsides covered with pine trees, the lower slopes terraced for the cultivation of olives, and the valley through which the line runs becomes increasingly steeper and narrower forcing the railway to twist and turn through the woods in order to find the easiest path. Soon afterwards two tunnels, both short in length, are encountered. Two kilometres beyond Bunyola the summit tunnel is reached, the line's highest altitude of 238.8 metres being attained about half way through. Further on, the line reaches a passing loop (added since 1988) and the platform where the daily Tourist Special pauses for ten minutes for the passengers to admire the view. The line is now on a steadily falling gradient and descends in a series of horseshoe curves round the lower slopes of the mountains. Ten more tunnels of varying lengths are passed on the descent, as well as a long viaduct. Eventually the resin-smelling pine woods of the summit give way once again to terraced cultivation and ultimately the line passes through lemon groves whose trees are so close to the train that one can almost pick the fruit from the carriage windows. Shortly after houses appear beside the track, and the line squeezes between them and a large running shed on the left to enter the station yard at Soller. This shed is shared by the railway's motor coaches and the trams that continue the journey down to the port. On the opposite side of the line is the old steam roundhouse and the line's workshops.

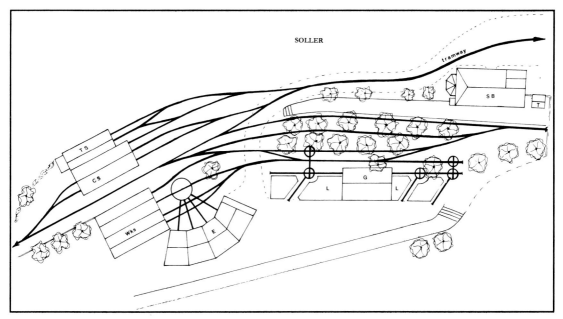

The station yard at Soller is planted with rows of plane trees, beneath which are several loop lines used for storing spare carriages. Across the yard from the station's only passenger platform is the old goods shed which, as usual with the FC de Soller, is only accessible by negotiating several wagon turntables. Passengers intending to catch the tram to the port descend an imposing stone stairway inside the station, a legacy of the building's former domestic use. Inside the hallway at street level one wall carries a plaque commemorating the opening of the railway.

General view of the station at Soller with the tracks shaded by plane trees.   (Author)

Wiring diagram of Soller station

after an original by Mr. H. Norman

▬▬	1200 v
●─●─●	600 v
───	1200/600 v
┼┼┼┼	Unwired
─╫─	Section gap
─┴─	Lifting Barrier
⊕	Voltage Indicator

Palma

Car-long Section Insulator

Puerto Soller

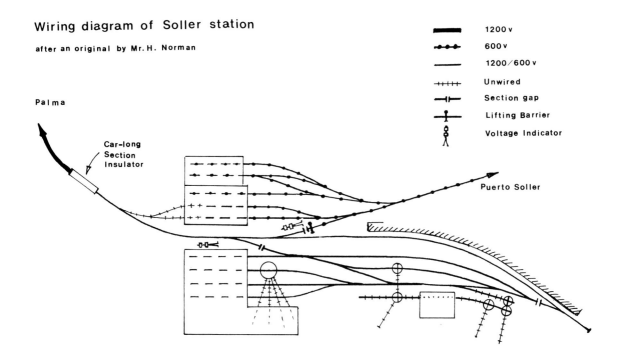

The Soller Tramway

From a running shed at the station throat several tracks combine to form a loop which is used by the tramcars to run round their trailers. This loop singles up behind the railway platform and the tramway drops steeply down to the street outside the station. Leaving this stop the tramway crosses a small Plaza, almost running between the tables of a pavement cafe before slipping into a side street. Here there is a loop line where the trailer cars are sometimes left while the tram continues alone to the station. A little further on to the left of the line is the site of a pair of sidings, one facing the station yard the other towards the port. The latter formerly served the local gas works and must have been the destination of a good deal of coal traffic. Shortly after this the line sqeezes between two houses to cross a side road which is the site of a request stop, following which the town's buildings are soon left behind and the line crosses the course of a small river by means of a substantial plate girder bridge, before dropping down a short, sharp incline. Travelling through the fields a passing loop is reached which is the mid-point fare stage of the line (shown on the tickets as Cruce), and shortly after this the main road to the port is encountered at an ungated level crossing. Some way further on is another loop line formerly used for goods traffic, and now partially lifted.

Road and rail continue in close proximity until at length the tramway is running along the top of the sea-wall round the Bay of Soller. The original terminus is marked by a loop line where the harbour jetty thrusts out into the bay, and there is a station incorporating a cafe situated on the seaward side of the line. In the 1920s a one kilometre extension was made along the street to serve the nearby Naval Base, but as there are no longer any run-round facilities available here the tramcars drop their trailers at the harbour station loop before continuing on to the end of the line alone. On the return journey a short halt is made to pick the trailers before the tram makes the return trip to Soller.

The tramway track is lighter than that used on the railway, and weighs only 22.7 kgs/metre. Double check rails are used where the line runs through the streets of Soller and at the port. For the majority of the run through the countryside normal sleepered track is used, though the ballasting and maintenance does not seem to be of a very high order. It is sufficient however for the light loads and low speeds employed.

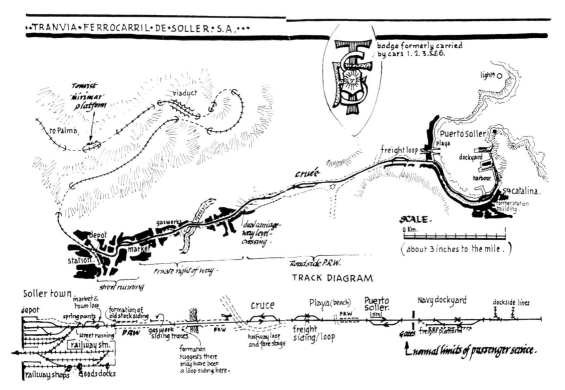

This charming map and diagram of the Soller Tramway was drawn by Herbert Norman, a lifelong 'Soller' enthusiast, now in his 90th year. A version of the map appeared in 'Modern Tramway' and is featured by kind permission of the Editor, Modern Tramway, now Light Rail and Modern Tramway, jointly published by the LRTA and Ian Allan Ltd.

A well-filled tram picks up more passengers on the outskirts of Soller, 11th July 1977.   (K. Taylorson)

Tram and open trailers running along the edge of the bay at Soller. January 1992.   (Author)

Tram No 3 at Puerto Soller.   (Author)

PART THREE: OTHER LINES

Chapter 10.
The Independent Railways and Tramways of Majorca

The Palma Tramways (1876 - 1959)

The Palma Tramways came into being with the Majorca Railway Company's desire to gain access to the harbour at Palma. As the city was already well established and no direct route was possible, it was found necessary to construct the link as an urban tramway through the streets of the capital.

Work started in February 1876 under the guidance of the railway's engineer, Eusebio Estada. The tramway emerged from the station and immediately turned to the right to run round the line of the old city walls to the Puetro de Jesús. From here it entered the city centre and passed down the Paseo de la Rambla and the Calle Navarra past the theatre where there was a sharp curve. It then ran along the Calle Unio (now known as Calle General Mola) where the line turned left to run southwards to the port along the Paseo del Borne and the Avenida Antonio Maura. This route opened in July 1876, using animal traction at first.

Another route opened to passengers in 1889. This ran south-east from the railway station before turning right at the Calle del Sindicato. From here it passed along the Calle Colon and through Plaza Cort to meet the other line at an area known as Glorieta (now Plaza de la Reina). At the same time the tramway was extended west along the harbour to serve the area round the Pueblo Español and continued beyond this to Santa Catalina.

The year 1889 was also marked by the company introducing a Nasmyth Wilson-built 0-4-0 tank engine to help move the increasing goods traffic. The mules had quickly learned that on curves it was best to step outside the line of the rails to haul the wagons round the bend, and it seems that the steam locomotive also tried to follow this example, one sharp curve in the Paseo del Borne being particularly troublesome. Apparently it soon became part of the local way of life for the citizens of Palma to help the railwaymen place the errant locomotive back on the track whenever this happened. Meanwhile passenger services on the Palma Tramways continued to be animal powered, mostly using open sided tramcars built by Carde y Escoriaza. These had canvas side screens to protect the passengers from the sun, and were generally hauled by two mules.

A few years later, possibly in 1891, the Santa Catalina line was extended to serve the suburb of Terreño and the new western harbour at Porto Pi. The order books of the Brush Electrical Engineering Company (the successors to Falcon) record that four tram engines (works nos 198-201) were supplied to the Palma Tramways and believed to be for this route. Their running numbers were 2 - 5. One (works no 198) was later transferred to the contractor building the FC de Soller, while the others appear to have faded away, unrecorded.

Although the railway company had introduced tramways to the centre of Palma, it is not certain during the early years whether the passenger tramcars were run by the FC de Mallorca or a separate organisation, Tranvías de Palma (Palma Tramways). However in 1914, following the successful electrification of the Soller Tramway the previous year, a company known as the Sociedad General de Tranvías Electricos Interurbanos de Palma de Mallorca (or T.E.I.P.) was formed in order to run, extend and electrify the Palma tramway system, and following three years' work the first electric tram ran on 27th June 1917.

To work the services the Tramway Company ordered a total of fifty tramcars. They were built by Carde y Escoriaza with electrical equipment by Siemens, of a type similar to those employed on the Soller Tramway with three-sided ends and straight sides. However at least one vehicle, motor-car 109 had rounded ends and a wider body whose lower side panels curved inwards towards the bogie frames. The running gear used French-built Brill trucks with a wheelbase of 2.2 metres, and the traction motors were rated at 35hp. Most of the old mule-tramcars were retained as trailers although four were acquired by the Soller Tramway in 1920. Not all the trailers were of the "toast-rack" type, as some had a closed body with end platforms. These vehicles are similar to the cars used from 1921 on the Arenal Tramway, making it a possibility that this undertaking also bought up some of the surplus trailers when the Palma system was electrified.

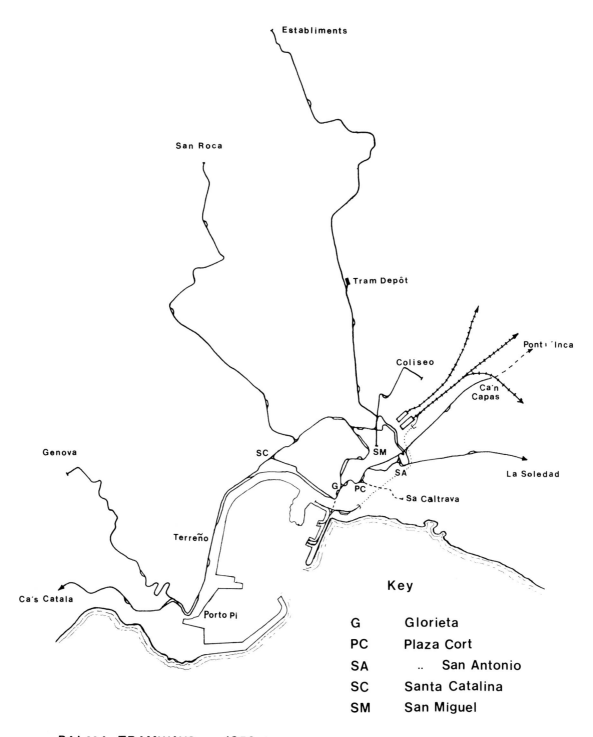

Establiments

San Roca

Tram Depôt

Coliseo

Pont⸱ Inca

Ca'n Capas

Genova

SC

SM

SA

La Soledad

G

PC

Sa Caltrava

Terreño

Ca's Catala

Porto Pi

Key

G	Glorieta
PC	Plaza Cort
SA	·· San Antonio
SC	Santa Catalina
SM	San Miguel

PALMA TRAMWAYS c. 1950

Tram and trailer in the Av. de Antonio Maura, Palma.   (collection J. Ibanez)

A collection of trams including a small enclosed trailer - possibly a survivor from mule-haulage days. This vehicle appears to be similar to the cars on the Arenal Tramway.   (collection J. Ibanez)

Palma tramcar No 38 on the Estaciones - Terreño route seen here at Glorieta. (L.G. Marshall)

Tramcar No 9 on the Porto Pi route on 9th October 1957. (A.W. Porter, courtesy J.H. Price)

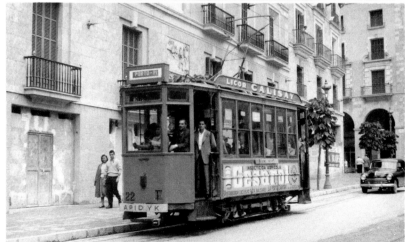

Tramcar No 22 on a rare length of double track in the centre of Palma. (L.G. Marshall)

Unhappily, the T.E.I.P's first day of service was marred by a fatal accident when the brakes failed on one of the tramcars in the Calle Conquistador and the runaway car crashed into a building in the Plaza de Isabel II. The tram appears to have been written off by this incident as later reports only mention forty nine cars in service. Over the next decade a total of ten new routes were opened, extending to over 50 kilometres of track by 1935. As well as the two original routes from the station to the harbour there was a new "outer circle" route to link the west end of the harbour with the original line. A new terminus was established near the market at San Miguel in the centre of the city, and from here a route ran northwards to the bull-ring (Coliseo). A branch off this line ran north of the city centre to Establiments and the tram depot was located on this branch at C'as Capiscol on the outskirts of the city.

From the Plaza San Antonio new lines were built including one which ran north-east to Pont d'Inca, meeting the FC de Mallorca's branch to Santany at a combined road, rail and tram crossing at C'an Capas. Another route ran eastwards to La Soledad on the main road to Manacor, while to the west of the city a branch line was taken off the "outer circle" to serve the outlying town of Son Roca. Beyond Porto Pi the coastal line was extended westwards to the seaside suburb of C'as Catala, while a branch from this route climbed into the hills to serve the nearby town of Genova. In addition it appears that prior to 1958 there was another branch in the city centre, running from Plaza Cort towards the Sa Caltrava district a short way to the east, possibly terminating in the Plaza San Francisco.

The tramway's success was paradoxically its own downfall. Many of the routes in the city centre ran through narrow streets where only a single track could be laid and consequently an intensive service in both directions was difficult to maintain, especially around the terminus at San Miguel and in the area round the railway stations where many routes converged. The longer routes were only single track with occasional passing loops - four on the Establiments line and three on the route to Son Roca, which must have made for fairly extended service intervals. The first closures came in 1954 on the outer end of the C'as Catala route which was cut back to terminate at Porto Pi.

An American visitor to Palma in March 1956 recorded his impressions of the local tramway system. The tramcars and track were by then in very poor condition and operations were conducted at a slow pace. At one spot on the Pont D'Inca route the rail had turned completely over on its side and the tram's wheels were running on the web of the rails for a short distance. Speed at this point was less than a walking pace, but even at normal speeds it was still possible to jump off a moving tram, run ahead to take a photograph, and then re-board the car as it caught up. Despite this state of affairs it was felt that much of the system would survive, if only because of the generally poor condition of the roads. In fact it was the Pont D'Inca line that was to suffer next when the line was cut back to terminate at C'an Capas, though this still left the routes serving Genova, Porto Pi, Establiments, Son Roca, Santa Catalina, Coliseo and Soledad. Some of the routes ran out into the country, and there were intermediate turn-round points on the longer routes (e.g. Railway Stations - Terreño on the Porto Pi route).

The scenery on the outermost limits could be spectacular. The Genova route climbed steeply up from the western end of the harbour with magnificent views over the city and the Bay of Palma. A series of sharp curves followed before the line reached an area of hill-top orchards and bluffs with Belver Castle in the background. Beyond the city, the lines to Establiments and Son Roca still ran along bucolic unpaved roads to reach the small picturesque towns at journey's end. Competing traffic (at least in the country districts) was mostly horse-drawn, even in the late 1950s.

Although buses had by now replaced some tram services little had been done to improve the roads, and in consequence the buses rode worse than the trams and were just as crowded and slow. Thus as late as 1956, when tram number 30 was modernised with a steamlined metal body, it still seemed possible that the network would survive. However this proved to be a false hope and by 1957 it was obvious that the Tramway's days were numbered as the track had deteriorated badly, in some places spreading out of gauge. This state of affairs could not continue and the company decided to implement the Alcover Plan (named after the President of the T.E.I.P.) under which the remaining tram routes were to be replaced by buses. March 16th 1958 saw the closure of the westerly routes which ran through the city centre and served Porto Pi, Genova, Santa Catalina and Son

Tramcar No 29 leaves Plaza San Antonio for Soledad shortly before closure. Even in the late 1950's there is little traffic. (J. Wiseman)

Tramcar No 30 (also known as "Marilyn Monroe" after her rebuild) seen on the Coliseo route shortly before closure. (J. Wiseman)

Roca, and by the end of the year the Soledad route had also changed to bus operation. This brought the number of operating trams down to 10, though their duties were now shared with buses on the remaining two routes (to Ca'n Capas and Establiments). Tram working was finally suspended early in 1959, and the rails removed from the streets.

The FC de Alaró (1881-1935)

There are a number of small coal mines near Alaró and the town had originally hoped to be on the FC de Mallorca's main line. However the railway company were unwilling to deviate from their planned direct route, and in consequence the FC de Alaró (Alaró Railway) was promoted independently to link the town with the main line at Consell station, just over two miles away. Construction began in 1880, and the line was opened on 22nd May 1881.

The promoters found money harder than expected to raise and although it had been hoped to provide steam locomotion there was only sufficient capital to provide two mule-hauled tramcars. One of these was a double-decker, built in Barcelona in 1880 with a capacity of forty three passengers, while the other was built in Palma a couple of years later and could carry 32 passengers. Two mules harnessed one behind the other were used to haul these cars and because of this loops were not necessary, the layout at the terminus consisting merely of three parallel tracks serving the passenger station, a carriage shed and the goods shed. At the junction, in the early days at least, there was another carriage shed, a goods loading bank situated on the siding connecting with the main line and a short stub siding. A stable for the mules was also provided.

Limited goods services were run for the benefit of the local coal mines, one of which was served by a private siding, while in later years a cement plant was established just outside the station at Alaró. FC de Mallorca wagons were used by the Alaró Railway and it is possible that they may have been moved by steam locomotives from the main line.

Early FC de Mallorca timetables did not include details of the Alaró services, though a timetable footnote read:- "Consell and Alaró. Between these two places there is a tramway 4 kilometres long, on which services are run connecting with trains on the Palma - Manacor line. Fares are 30 cents 1st Class, 20 cents 2nd Class." Journey times were 15 minutes on the mainly uphill journey to Alaró, and 10 minutes in the reverse direction.

The line seems to have been a success, initially at least, as in 1922 mule-haulage was replaced by two 18 hp petrol driven railmotors. These appear to have had flat-bed bodies, capable of carrying a couple of tonnes of goods, and were presumably used to haul the tramcars, though this would have needed the provision of run round loops at each end of the line.

The railmotors had been bought with money raised by a further share issue, and after their introduction there was little surplus cash to run the tramway. The situation worsened in 1923 when some of the local mines closed, while at the same time road transport began to provide serious competition. Both the trackwork and the two tramcars were in a bad state of repair by the beginning of the 1930s and the directors approached the FC de Mallorca in the hope of merging the two companies. The offer was declined and on 30th May 1935 the Alaró Railway was closed "provisionally". The economic climate that resulted from the Civil War ensured that the closure became permanent, and the track was lifted in 1941.

During the last few years further details of the tramway had appeared in the FC de Mallorca timetables. Services left Alaró at 5.35am, 7.35, and 8.55; 1.00pm, 2.15, 3.00 and 6.55 with an extra departure on Sundays and Holidays at 8.30pm. Homeward trips from Consell ran at 8.15am and 9.15, 2.45pm, 3.45 and 7.40 with a final run at 8.55pm on Sundays and Holidays. These late runs connected with the last train out of Palma, which was held back from its weekday departure of 6.50pm to leave at 8.10pm - arriving at Consell at 8.55pm. Normally the tramway journeys took 15 minutes, but for some reason an extra five minutes was allowed at the weekend.

Later, between 1944 and 1951, part of the branch was reinstated as a long siding to serve the local mines, but after this the tracks were again lifted. Today little remains to identify the route of the line.

The Arenal Tramway (1921 - 1935)

Another independant line, known locally as the Carrilet de S'Arenal (Arenal Tramway), formerly ran along part of the Bay of Palma. Promoted in 1921 by Señor José Fontirroig, the line originally linked Arenal with a terminus near the former Café La Sirena in C'an Pastilla but was soon extended a couple of kilometres westward to serve Coll d'En Rabassa. Work on the tramway proceeded quickly as there were no natural obstacles to be overcome, and the line was lightly laid with flat-bottomed rail spiked to the sleepers. Today the site of the tramway is a concrete promenade, but in former times it was an unspoiled beach with no development apart from the two small towns at either end.

The opening ceremony, which took place on 14th October 1921, was described in flowery terms in the local newspaper, which made much of the beautiful views to be seen from the line, both looking inland and along the bay. The inaugural service left Coll d'En Rabassa to the pealing of the local church bells. On board were José Fontirroig and the other members of the Tramway's governing body. A short stop was made at C'an Pastilla before the tram moved on through a large crowd who lined both sides of the track so closely that the speed had to be kept to a crawl. The arrival at Arenal was also met with the acclamation of the local populace, while the town band from Lluchmayor struggled to make itself heard above the din. A welcoming committee consisting of the Mayor and Secretary of the Town Council together with the Civil Guard lieutenant and the parish priest met the tram, which was blessed on its arrival. After this, the band led the crowd to the church for a Te Deum which was followed by an inspection of the Tramway depot where refereshments were taken, the crowd serenaded all the while by the Lluchmayor musicians. In the speeches that followed the Mayor of Lluchmayor congratulated his Arenal collegue on the opening of the line and expressed the hope that the tramway might soon be extended to link Arenal with Lluchmayor. However, although plans for this scheme were drawn up the following year, and a share issue announced, the work never progressed any further.

At first the timetable was ambitious, with departures from Arenal at 6.00am, 7.15, 8.15, 10.15, 11.00 and then hourly until 6.00pm with a final service at 7.30 in the evening. Return trips were scheduled at 6.30am, 8.00, 9.30, 11.00 and then every hour until 7.00pm with the final run being made at 8.30pm. A brief examination of these timings indicates the existence of at least two sets of tramcars, and this is confirmed by a picture in the writer's collection showing the depot at Arenal. It shows a substantial building constructed from reinforced concrete to a traditional design, with three arched entrances for rolling stock - considerably more than would have been required by a "one car" operation. As well as housing the tramcars it also provided workshop facilities for light repairs as well as living quarters for a night-watchman.

The services were maintained by petrol driven railcars having a 12hp Citroen engine. These vehicles resembled a single deck horse tram and may indeed have been converted from old mule-hauled trams from the

An Artists impression of an Arenal Tramway Car (Author)

Palma system, which had been electrified a short time previously. The tramcar's roof overhung the body at both ends, and was fitted with a clerestory roof above the passenger compartment. Access was by means of a rear platform and the engine was mounted at the front in place of a platform. The chassis appeared very solid in construction, and the four wheels were set close together, slightly forward of the car's centre line. The passenger compartment had five windows on each side with three windows facing forward, and two windows and a glazed door to the rear. A trailer coach was also used; this was generally similar but had a platform at both ends. As the railcars were single-ended it is assumed that there was a "balloon loop" or a turntable at each end of the run.

Although the Lluchmayor extension remained unbuilt, by 1926 the tramway appears to have been extended as far as the outer edge of Palma, where a connection was made with the Palma Tramways at the Plaza San Antonio. This combined tram journey was a more convenient way of travelling between Arenal and Palma than by railway, nevertheless services seem to have declined in later years, possibly due to the establishment of a competing bus service, without the need to change vehicles. During the 1930s there were only six return trips daily, and while the tram trailers may have been more widely used at first, eventually they were only needed on Sundays and public holidays.

This interesting and little known line closed in 1937 and the tracks were lifted. Subsequent development has covered all traces of the line.

Genova Quarries

Finally, there was yet one more railway undertaking on the island. This was an industrial line which linked a quarry at Genova, a short way west of Palma, with the western quays of the harbour. The gauge was the Majorcan "standard" of 3 feet. The quarry owned several locomotives but they all appear to have been scrapped or sold some time after September 1954. Known details suggest that there were two 0-6-0 tanks numbered L2 and L9, an unknown engine, possibly a rebuild by Construcciones Devis SA of Valencia, an 0-4-0 by Orenstein & Koppel numbered L18, plus others whose details are lost. It is possible to speculate that this line might have been the final resting place for the three "missing" Falcon locomotives, as no evidence exists that they went to either the Arenal or Alaró lines after 1917, though either might have been logical in theory. A visitor to the island in 1958 reports that by then the quarry line had been lifted, but despite this it seems to have survived, on some maps at least, until the mid 1970s.

Other Projected Lines
The North Majorcan Railway

The period just before the First World War was a time of great railway enthusiasm in Majorca, when current projects included the construction of the FC de Soller and the planning of the Santany branch by the FC de Mallorca. In August 1912 a proposal was made for a line running northwards from Inca, via Selva and Campanet, to reach Pollensa and Alcudia. The two ports associated with these towns would be served by short branch lines. From Alcudia it was planned to head southwards to link up with the FC de Mallorca at La Puebla.

Although a three year construction period was agreed and the contract for this 54 kilometre extension was awarded, the original promoter ran into difficulties and in December 1912 the scheme was ceded to the Compañia del Ferrocarril del Norte de Mallorca (North Majorca Railway). The foundation stone for Pollensa station was laid shortly after this, and some land donated for the planned route, but the scheme never progressed further, presumably falling victim to the supply difficulties during the war and the rise of motor transport afterwards.

At various times the FC de Mallorca attempted to extend its La Puebla branch towards Alcudia, and at one time it was estimated that some 60% of the trackbed had been completed, though the lines never went beyond the far end of La Puebla itself. The coastal area of this part of the island is now a major holiday resort, and if the branch was to be re-opened in the future it could be a useful asset for the locality.

Comparatively recently proposals were studied for a rail link to Cala Millor using part of the Arta branch but as this would have needed a very high capital investment, the scheme was dropped.

ANNEXE

Other Balearic Railways

Although the second largest Balearic Island, Minorca, has no railway, both Ibiza and Formentera were once provided with industrial lines. These belonged to La Salinera Española SA (Spanish Saltworks Company) and had a gauge of 750mm.

Originally the company employed steam power in the shape of several 0-4-0 tank engines built by Decauville at their Petit-Bourg workshops. This company built standard engines in three sizes, and eventually the saltworks owned at least one of each type, though other locomotives have also been recorded. As steam power was used from 1896 to 1966 some of the earlier locomotives may not have survived, although it seems that two were in use on each island.

The Formentera system employed No.2 (Decauville No 242 - ordered 6.8.1896, delivered 12.10.1896). This was a 3 tonne locomotive similar to those working the Volos narrow gauge line in Greece. Also in use was No 3, an Orenstein & Koppel of unknown date. After 1966 the steam engines were laid aside and replaced by two Maffei 4-wheeled diesels. These were painted in a red and blue livery and one engine carried the number 2. One locomotive worked at each end of the line shunting wagons, while main line trips were headed by a road tractor which straddled the rails.

On Ibiza the former steam locomotives were both by Decauville. Works No 231 (ordered 16.12.1897, delivered 9.2.1898) was a 5 tonne engine which was given the running number 3. The other locomotive had been obtained second-hand from the Compañía Arrendataria de las Salinas de Torrevieja (Torrevieja Salt Company) on the Spanish mainland. It carried the name SALAS II No 6 and was a 7.5 tonne engine originally ordered on 24.4.1899 and delivered to its original owners on 14.1.1900. After 1966 the line line was worked by three Deutz 4-wheeled diesels, works numbers 55689/90 (built 1958) and 57078. All were rated at 28 hp and carried a green livery. The working method was the opposite to Formentera, as the diesels worked the short main line, while tractors performed the shunting duties.

Both railways were phased out in the early 1970's and few traces now remain.

The 0-4-0 wing tank tentatively identified as Decauville 242/1897 dumped at the site of the saltworks railway on Formentera, July 1974.
(R.N. Redman)

APPENDIX I
Ferrocarriles de Mallorca Motive Power list
Steam Locomotives

(a/date) last year locomotive still known to be active

(d/date) month/year known to be derelict/withdrawn from service

rn   rebuilt and renumbered (new number given if known)

w   date recorded withdrawn from service

NW= Nasmyth Wilson;   MTM= La Maquinista;   OK= Orenstein & Koppel

P= Palma Works;   K=Krupp;   BW= Babcock & Wilcox

Number	Name	Maker	Type	Dates	Remarks
1	MAJORCA	NW	4-4-0T	1874-1945	
2	PALMA	NW	4-4-0T	1874-c1948	
3	INCA	NW	4-4-0T	1874-c1955	
4	MANACOR	NW	0-6-0T	1876-1960	(a1957)
5	FELANITX	NW	0-6-0T	1876-1960	(a1957)
6(i)	SINEU	NW	4-4-0T	1877-1911	rn
6(ii)	-	NW	0-4-0T	c1917-c1955	"LA INGLESITA"
7(i)	LA PUEBLA	NW	2-2-0T	1877-1911	rn
7(ii)	-	OK	0-4-0WT	1921-c1960	carried no number after 1944
7(iii)	-	MTM	2-6-0T	1944-c1960	(a1957) exFC Soller
8(i)	SANTA MARIA	NW	4-4-0T	1877-1911	rn
8(ii)	-	MTM	2-6-0T	1944-c1960	(d 6/60) exFC Soller
9(i)	BINISALEM	NW	4-4-0T	1877-1911	rn
9(ii)	-	MTM	2-6-0T	1944-c1960	(d 6/60) ex FC Soller
10(i)	MURO	NW	4-4-0T	1881-1911	rn
10(ii)	SANTA EUGENIA	NW	4-6-0T	c1917-c1960	(d 6/60)
11(i)	PETRA	NW	4-4-0T	1881-1929	rn 18
11(ii)	ALGAIDA	NW	4-6-0T	1929-c1960	(a1955) (d 6/60)
12	SAN JUAN	NW	4-6-0T	1887-c1960	(d 6/60)
13	LLOSETA	NW	4-6-0T	1891-c1960	(a1957) (d 6/60)
14	MARRATXI	NW	4-6-0T	1891-c1960	(d6/60)
15	ALARO	NW	4-6-0T	1891-c1960	(a1957)
16	PORRERAS	NW	4-6-0T	1897-1960	(a1960) (d 6/60)
17	MONTUIRI	NW	4-6-0T	1897-c1955	
18(i)	ALFONSO XIII	P	4-4-0T	1902-c1911	rn 22/re-named
18(ii)	ALGAIDA	NW	4-6-0T	c1917-1929	rn 11
18(iii)	PETRA	NW	4-4-0T	1929-c1960	(d 6/60)
19(i)	ESPAÑA	P	4-4-0T	1903-c1911	rn 23

19(ii)	LLUCHMAYOR	MTM	2-6-0T	1917-c1960	(a1955/57) (w by 6/60)
20(i)	ALGAIDA	NW	4-6-0T	1911-c1917	rn 18
20(ii)	CAMPOS	MTM	2-6-0T	1917-c1960	(a1953/57)
21(i)	SANTA EUGENIA	NW	4-6-0T	1911-c1917	rn 10
21(ii)	SANTANY	MTM	2-6-0T	1917-c1960	(a1960)
22	SALINAS	P	4-4-0T	c1911-c1960	(a1955/57) (d by 6/60)
23	ESPAÑA	P	4-4-0T	c1911-c1955	
24	COLL	P	4-4-0T	1911-1960	(a1957) (d6/60)
25	SAN MIGUEL	P	4-4-0T	1911-c1955	
26	SAN LLORENZO	P	4-4-0T	1911-c1955	
27	ARTA	P	4-4-0T	1911-c1960	(a1953/57) (d 6/60)
28	SON SERVERA	P	4-4-0T	1911-c1955	
30 - 35	-	K	2-6-0T	1926-c1964	
50 - 55	-	BW	2-6-2T	1930-c1964	

(numbers 24 to 28 were rebuilt from numbers 6 to 10)

FC de Mallorca Railcars

No.	Type	Rating	Engine Type		Builder	Dates	Notes
A1	4-wheel	40hp	petrol mechanical		Berliet	1926 - 1936	(d6/60)
A2	4-wheel	40hp	"	"	De Dion/CAF	1930 - c1970	
A3	4-wheel	40hp	"	"	" "	1930 - c1970	
A4	4-wheel	40hp	"	"	" "	1930 - c1970	

FEVE Bogie Railcars

No.	Builder	Date	Arrival on island	In use from	Departure/ disposal	Notes
2001	Esslingen	1956	1956	1956	19.07.66	f
2002	"	"	1956	1956	?w 1991	
2003	"	"	1956	1956	w by 1979	f
2004	"	"	1956	1956	?w 1991	
2005	Euskalduna	1959	1959	1959	?w 1991	
2006	"	1960	1960	1960	?w 1991	
2009	"	1959	1959		w by 1979	
2011	"	1958	1958		wby1979	ob 12/91
2012	"	1958	1979	r		
2013	"		c1980	r		ob 12/91
2019	"	1959	1959	1966	?w 1991	
2020	"	1959	c1980	r		
2026	"	1959	1969	1971	19.05.73	f

2027	"	1960	1969	1973	?w 1991
2028	"		c1980	r	
2029	"		c1980	r	
2360)	MAN	1984	1991	1991	-
2365)					
23xx)	MAN	1984	1991	1991	-
23xx)					

w = withdrawn   f = destroyed by fire r = awaiting rebuilding/gauge conversion
ob = seen with body removed from bogies

FEVE Railcar Trailers

No.	Builder	Date	Arrival on Island	In use from	Departure/ disposal	Notes
5001*	Esslingen	1956	1956	1956		
5002**	"	"	"	"		?d by 1991
5003*	"	"	"	"		?d by 1991 "
5004*	"	"	"	"		
5005*	"	"	"	"		
5006						
5011			c1980	r		
5012			c1980			
5013			c1980	r		?d by 1991
5015			c1980	r		?d by 1991
5016			c1980	r		
5017						
5018+						?d by 1991
5019			c1980	r		?d by 1991

* = fitted with toilet & postal compartment until c 1980
** = "   "   "   "   "   "   " c 1989
+ = short trailer

FEVE Diesel Locomotives

No	Type	Builder	Date	Arrival on Island	In Use From	Withdrawn	Notes
1101)	B-B		1958	1959	1959	c. 1974	)
1102)	Diesel	S.E.C.N.	1958	1959	1959	c. 1968	) 3ft
1103)	Hydraulic		1958	1959	1959	c. 1974	) gauge
1104)			1958	1959	1960	c. 1968	)
1207	0-6-0	Batignolles/CAF	1960	c.1980	1981		metre gauge

APPENDIX II
Locomotive Dimensions

	4-4-0T	4-4-0T	4-4-0T	0-6-0T	4-6-0T
	MAJORCA PALMA INCA	SINEU LA PUEBLA STA MARIA BINISALEM	MURO PETRA PORRERAS MONTUIRI ALFONSO/ SALINAS plus 1911 rebuilds	MANACOR FELANITX	SAN JUAN LLOSETA MARRATXI ALARO ALGAIDA STA EUGENIA
Cylinders diam/stroke	11"x18" 0.279x0.457	13"x18" 0.330x0.457	13.5"x19" 0.342x0.48	13"x18" 0.330x0.457	15"x20" 0.381x0.508
Leading wheels	2' 0" 0.610	2' 0" 0.610	2' 0" 0.610	none -	2' 0" 0.610
Coupled wheels	3' 6" 1.067	3' 6" 1.067	3' 6" 1.067	3' 3" 0.990	3' 3" 0.990
Coupled w/base	6' 9" 2.057	7' 9" 2.362	7' 9" 2.362	12' 6" 3.810	12' 1" 3.684
Total w/base	14' 10" 4.520	16' 4.5" 4.991	16' 4.5" 4.991	12' 6" 3.810	19' 5.5" 5.930
Length over buffers	23' 7.5" 7.200	26' 3" 8.000	26' 3" 8.000	24' 10.5" 7.583	29' 0.5" 8.850
Boiler length	8' 0" 2.438	8' 0" 2.438	8' 9" 2.667	8' 9" 2.667	10' 3" 3.125
Boiler diameter	3' 0" 0.915	3' 0" 0.915	3' 5.5" 1.053	3' 5.5" 1.053	3' 7" 1.095
Firebox length	3' 6" 1.067	3' 6" 1.067	3' 9" 1.143	3' 7.5" 1.105	4' 8.5" 1.425
Smokebox length	1' 11.5 0.600	2' 1" 0.638	2' 2.5" 0.675	2' 2.5" 0.675	2' 2.5" 0.675
Weight	15.8t	16.3t	see text	16.2t	

	2-6-0T Maquinista	2-6-0T Krupp	2-6-2T Babcock & Wilcox	0-4-0T Nasmyth Wilson	0-4-0T O & K
Cyls diam/stroke	14.25"x19.75" 0.360x0.500	14.5"x20.75" 0.370x0.530	14.5"x21.6" 0.370x0.550	10"x14" 0.254x0.356	
Leading wheels	2'3.9" 0.710	2' 3.9" 0.710	2' 3.9" 0.710	none	none
Coupled wheels	3' 5" 1.041	3' 7.25" 1.100	3' 7.25" 1.100	2' 6" 0.762	
Rear wheels	none	none	2' 3.9" 0.710	none	none
Coupled w/base	8' 2.5" 2.500	9' 6.25" 2.900	9' 4.25" 2.850	5' 0" 1.524	
Total w/base	15' 1.1" 4.600	16' 4.8" 5.000	21' 11.75" 6.700	5' 0" 1.524	
Length over buffers	28' 4.5" 8.649	28' 11" 8.815	33' 4" 10.160	16' 8.75" 5.100	18' 4.5" 5.600
Boiler length	10' 6" 3.200	9' 10.1" 3.000	11' 9.8" 3.630	5' 9" 1.753	
Boiler diam	3' 9.75" 1.163	3' 11.25" 1.200	3' 11.25" 1.200	3' 1" 0.940	
Firebox length	5' 2" 1.575	3' 5.25" 1.050	3' 11.25" 1.200	3' 8" 1.118	
Smokebox length	3' 2.25" 0.975	4' 2.25" 1.275	4' 11" 1.500	1' 8.6" 0.525	
Weight	30.75t	37.3t	46.4t	12.5t	13.2t

APPENDIX III

PALMA Á MANACOR

PRECIOS 1.ª c.	2.ª c.	3.ª	K.	ESTACIONES.	2 1ª 2ª	4 1ª 2 3	6 1ª 2 3	10 1ª 2ª	8 1.ª 2 3
P. C.	P. C.	P. C.							
»	»	»	»	PALMA.................. S...	7.40	14. »	14. 3	18.16	14.40
0.55	0.30	»	4	Pont d'Inca..................	7.50	14.10	14.13	18.27	14.50
0.80	0.45	»	9	Marratxi..................	8. 5	14.25	14.28	18.45	15. 5
1.20	0.75	0.55	15	Santa María (E.)..................	8.24	14.44	14.46	19.10	15.24
1.55	0.95	0.65	19	Consell (E.).............. Ll..	8.34	14.54		19.20	15.34
				S...	8.35	14.55		19.21	15.35
1.75	1.10	0.70	22	Binisalen..................	8.44	15. 4		19.30	15.44
2.05	1.25	0.85	26	Lloseta..................	8.51	15.11		19.37	15.51
2.15	1.35	1.00	29	Inca..................	9. 1	15.21		19.47	16. 1
2.75	1.75	1.15	34	Son Bordils (E.).............. Ll..	9.11	15.31		19.57	16.11
				S...	9.16	15.32		20. 2	
3.15	2.00	1.35	43	Sineu..................	9.34	15.50		20.39	
3.25	2.10	1.35	45	San Juan..................	9.41	15.57		20.48	
3.65	2.30	1.35	54	Petra..................	9.55	16.11		21.15	
4.00	2 55	1.35	64	MANACOR.............. Ll..	10.10	16.26		21.40	

					1 1ª 2 3	3 1ª 2 3	5 1ª 2ª	9 1ª 2ª	7 1.ª 2 3
»	»	»	»	MANACOR.............. S...	2.30	6.30		17.15	
0.85	0.55	»	10	Petra..................	3.10	6.49		17.34	
1.60	1.05	»	19	San Juan..................	3.40	7. 5		17.50	
1.70	1.10	»	21	Sineu..................	4. »	7.14		17.59	
2.40	1.60	»	30	Son Bordils (E.).............. Ll..	4.25	7.29		18.14	
				S...	4.30	7.34	12.50	18.19	
2.75	1.85	»	35	Inca..................	5.15	7.48	13. 4	18.33	
3.05	2.05	»	38	Lloseta..................	5.38	7.58	13 14	18.43	
3.25	2.25	»	42	Binisalen..................	5.53	8. 6	13.22	18 51	
3.50	2.30	»	45	Consell (E.).............. Ll..	6.15	8.15	13.31	19. »	
					6.18	8.16	13.32	19. 1	
3.55	2.40	»	49	Santa María (E.)..................	6.33	8.25	13.41	19.10	14.46
4.00	2.55	»	56	Marratxi..................	6.56	8.40	13.56	19.26	15. 4
4.00	2.55	»	60	Pont d'Inca..................	7.10	8.52	14.12	19.37	15.16
4.00	2.55	1.35	64	PALMA.............. Ll.	7.30	9. »	14.20	19.45	15.24

Los sábados sale de Manacor para Palma un tren á las 11.55 y de Palma para Manacor á las 4.45 tarde.

CONSELL Á ALARÓ

Entre estos dos puntos hay un tranvía de 4 kilómetros de extensión, por el que circulan trenes ascendentes y descendentes en combinación con la línea de Palma á Manacor, y cuyos asientos cuestan 30 ó 20 céntimos, según sean de 1.ª ó 2.ª clase.

SON BORDILS Á LA PUEBLA

PRECIOS 1.ª c.	2.ª c.	K.	ESTACIONES.	18 1-2	20 1-2-3	22 1-2
»	»	»	SON BORDILS (E.).................. S...	9.16	16.12	20. 2
0.60	0.45	5	Llubi..................	9.27	16.23	20.20
0.80	0.55	9	Muro..................	9.36	16.32	20.33
1.05	0.75	13	LA PUEBLA.................. Ll..	9.44	16.40	20.41
				17 1-2-3	17 1-2	21 1ª 2ª
»	»	»	LA PUEBLA.................. S...	6.55	12. »	17.25
0.55	0.35	4	Muro..................	7. 4	12.15	17.40
0.75	0.50	8	Llubi..................	7.15	12.33	17.58
1.05	0.75	13	SON BORDILS (E.).................. Ll..	7.25	12.45	18.10

SANTA MARIA Á FELANITX

PRECIOS 1.ª c.	2.ª c.	K.	ESTACIONES.	12 1-2	14 1-2-3	16 1ª 2ª
»	»	»	SANTA MARÍA (E.).................. S...	8.24	14.47	19.19
0.70	0.45	7	Santa Eugenia..................	8.39	15. 2	19.30
1.20	0.80	16	Algaida..................	9. 2	15.25	20. 3
1.80	1.20	23	Montuiri..................	9.18	15.41	20.26
2.40	1.55	30	Porreras..................	9.34	15.57	20.49
2.85	1.80	36	Las Canteras..................	9.47	16.10	21. 9
3.35	2.10	43	FELANITX.................. Ll..	10. 4	16.27	21.27
				11 1ª 2 3	13 1ª 2ª	15 1ª 2ª
»	»	»	FELANITX.................. S...	6.40	12.15	17. »
0.70	0.45	7	Las Canteras..................	6.55	12.35	17.18
1.05	0.75	18	Porreras..................	7.12	13. »	17.41
1.65	1.10	20	Montuiri..................	7.30	13.27	18. 3
2.30	1.50	27	Algaida..................	7.49	13.55	18.31
2.85	1.85	36	Santa Eugenia..................	8. 6	14.18	18.50
3.35	2.10	43	SANTA MARÍA (E.).................. Ll..	8.20	14.32	19. 5

1913

PALMA A ARTA, A FELANITX Y A LA PUEBLA

PRECIOS 1.ª	2.ª	3.ª	K.	ESTACIONES	4-82 1-2	6-52 1-2	10-54 1-2	8 1-2	16-56 1-2	6-62 1-2	14-64 1-2	12-64 1-2	16-66 1-2	2 2-3
P. C.	P. C.	P. C.												
Desde Palma.			»	*PALMA.......... S..	8. »	8.25	14.15	13.45	18.30	8.25	14.45	14.35	18.30	7.15
0,55	0,30	»	4	Pont d'Inca..........	»	»	»	13.55	18 38	»	»	»	18.38	7.22
0,80	0,40	»	9	Marratxí..........	»	8.41	»	14. 9	18 47	8.41	»	»	18.47	7.31
1,25	0,75	0,60	15	*SANTA MARIA.. L.	8.20	8.59	14.45	14.24	18.59	8.59	»	»	18.59	7.39
				S..	8.22			14 25		9. 4	»	»	19. »	7.40
1,60	0,95	0,70	19	*CONSELL..........	»			14.35		9.14	15.25	»	19. 7	7.47
1,80	1,15	0,75	22	Binisalem..........	8.33			14.45		9.23	15.35	»	19.14	7.54
2,10	1,30	0,90	26	Lloseta..........	»			14.52		9.30	15.42	»	19.21	8. 1
2,25	1,40	1,05	29	Inca..........	8.45			15. »		2.39	15.51	15.20	19.28	8. 8
2,85	1,80	1,20	34	*EMPALME...... Ll.	»			—		9.48	15.59	»	19.36	—
				S..	»			—				»	19.37	—
3,25	2,05	1,40	43	Sineu..........	9 6			—				15.41	19.50	—
3,35	2,15	1,40	45	San Juan..........	9.12			—				15.47	19.55	—
3,75	2,25	1,40	54	Petra..........	9 24			—				16. »	20. 5	—
4,10	2,60	1,40	64	MANACOR..........	9.43			—				16.20	20.17	—
5,00	3,20	1,80	73	San Lorenzo..........	9.57			—				16.34	—	—
5,25	3,35	1,90	77	San Miguel..........	10. 3			—				16.40	—	—
5,95	3,85	2,20	84	Son Servera..........	10.14			—				16.51	—	—
6,85	4,45	2,60	94	Artá.......... Ll.	10.28			—				17. 5	—	—
Desde Santa María.								—						
»	»	»	»	*SANTA MARIA.. S.	—	9. 5	14.46	—	19. 1			—		—
0,70	0,45	»	7	Santa Eugenia..........	—	9.17	15. 1	—	19.14			—		—
1,25	0,80	»	16	Algaida..........	—	9.36	15.22	—	19.34			—		—
1,85	1,25	»	23	Montuiri..........	—	9.50	15.35	—	19.49			—		—
2,50	1,60	»	30	Porreras..........	—	10. 4	15.50	—	20. 4			—		—
2,95	1,85	»	36	Las Canteras..........	—	10.16	16. 2	—	20.17			—		—
3,45	2,15	»	43	FELANITX...... Ll.	—	10.31	16.18	—	20.33			—		—
Desde Empalme.					—			—						—
»	»	»	»	*EMPALME...... S..	—	—	—	—	—	9.49	16. »	—	19.38	—
0,60	0,45	»	5	Lluví..........	—	—	—	—	—	9.59	16. 9	—	19.51	—
0,80	0,55	»	9	Muro..........	—	—	—	—	—	10. 9	16.18	—	20. 6	—
1,10	0,75	»	13	LA PUEBLA..... Ll.	—	—	—	—	—	10.18	16.26	—	20.15	—

TREN número 16-66.—Los domingos y días festivos, retrasa su salida de Palma hasta las 20.

LA PUEBLA, FELANITX Y MANACOR A PALMA

PRECIOS 1.ª	2.ª	3.ª	K.	ESTACIONES	1 1-2-3	81-5 1-2	13 1-2-3	9 1-2	85-15 1-2	51-3 1-2	53-11 1-2	55-15 1-2	61-3 1-2	63-11 1-2	65-15 1-2
P. C.	P. C.	P. C.													
Desde La Puebla															
»	»	»	»	LA PUEBLA ...S..	—	—	—	—	—	—	—	—	7. »	12.15	17.15
0,55	0,35	»	4	Muro..........	—	—	—	—	—	—	—	—	7.10	12.27	17.31
0,75	0,50	»	8	Llubí..........	—	—	—	—	—	—	—	—	7.20	12.39	17 50
1,10	0,75	»	13	*EMPALME... Ll.	—	—	—	—	—	—	—	—	7.30	12.48	18. 3
Desde Felanitx															
»	»	»	»	FELANITX.. S..	—	—	—	—	—	6.45	11.50	17.15			
0,70	0,45	»	7	Las Canteras......	—	—	—	—	—	6.59	12. 4	17.29			
1,10	0,75	»	18	Porreras..........	—	—	—	—	—	7.16	12.19	17.44			
1,70	1,15	»	20	Montuiri..........	—	—	—	—	—	7.32	12.34	17.59			
2,40	1,55	»	27	Algaida..........	—	—	—	—	—	7.50	12.51	18.15			
2,95	1,90	»	36	Santa Eugenia.....	—	—	—	—	—	8. 5	13. 7	18.31			
3,45	2,15	»	43	*STA. MARIA. Ll.	—	—	—	—	—	8.19	13.27	18.45			
Desde Artá															
»	»	»	»	Artá........ S..	—	8.50	—	—	16. »						
1,20	0,60	0,40	10	Son Servera.......	—	7. 5	—	—	16.19						
1,60	1,05	0,70	17	San Miguel........	—	7.16	—	—	16.40						
1,85	1,25	0,80	21	Natá Lorenzo......	—	7.23	—	—	16·50						
2,75	1,85	1,20	30	MANACOR........	5.25	7.42	—	—	17.15						
3,60	2,40	»	40	Petra..........	5.38	8. 1	—	—	17.33						
4,40	2,95	»	49	San Juan..........	5.48	8.14	—	—	17.45						
4,50	3,00	»	51	Sineu..........	5.53	8.20	—	—	17.52						
5,25	3,50	»	60	*EMPALME... Ll.	»	»	—	—	18. 5						
				S..	»	»	—	—	18.10				7.31	12.49	18.10
5,60	3,75	»	65	Inca..........	6.14	8.43	17. »	11.30	18.19				7.48	13. »	18.20
5,90	3,95	»	68	Lloseta..........	6.20	»	17. 7	11.37	18.26				7.58	13. 7	18.28
6,10	4,15	»	72	Binisalem..........	6.26	8.54	17.14	11.44	18.33				8. 5	13.14	18.33
6,35	4,20	»	75	Consell..........	6.33	»	17.21	11.51	18.40				8.14	13.21	18.40
6,40	4,30	»	79	*STA. MARIA. Ll.	6.38	9. 4	17.27	11.57	18.46				8.22	13.27	18.48
				S..	6.39	9. 5	17.28	11.58	18.50	8.27	13.29	18.50	8.27	13.29	18.50
6,85	4,45	»	86	Marratxí..........	6.48	»	17.37	»	»	8.40	13.40	»	8.41	13.40	»
6,85	4,45	»	90	Pont d'Inca........	6.55	»	17.46	»	»	8.50	13.49	»	8.50	13.49	»
6,85	4,45	2,60	94	*PALMA...... Ll.	7. »	9.25	17.52	12.20	19.12	8.58	13.55	19.12	8.58	13.55	19.12

TREN 81-5.—Los viajeros cuyo destino sea el Empalme, se apearán en Inca, los que vayan a Lloseta lo harán en Benisalem y los que a Conseil en Santa María para tomar el tren 6. Los que vayan a Marratxí y Pont d'Inca se apearán en Santa María para tomar el tren 7.—TREN 53-11.—Circulan los martes, miércoles, viernes, sábados y domingos.—TREN 85-15.—Los viajeros cuyo destino sea Marratxí o Pont d'Inca se apearán en Santa María para tomar el tren 17.

1934

PALMA A SANTAÑY

PRECIOS 1.ª	2.ª	3.ª	K.	ESTACIONES	72 1-2	74 Cor. 1-2-3	76 Mix. 1-2		
P. C.	P. C.	P. C.							
»	»	»	»	*PALMA.......................... S..	7.55	14.40	18.25	—	—
0,40	0,25	0,15	6	Coll d'en Rebassa..........................	8. 6	14.50	18.36	—	—
0,95	0,60	0,35	14	El Arenal..........................	8.24	15. 2	18.51	—	—
2,00	1,25	0,75	30	Lluchmayor..........................	9. 2	15.26	19.25	—	—
3,15	1,85	1,15	44	Campos..........................	9.28	15.45	19.56	—	—
3,50	2,10	1,30	52	Baños de San Juan..........................	9.44	15.57	20.12	—	—
3,75	2,25	1,35	55	Las Salinas..........................	9.50	16. 3	20.23	—	—
4,00	2,60	1,40	62	SANTAÑY.......................... Ll.	10. »	16.12	20.33	—	—

TREN número 76.—Circula los jueves.
Trenes sólo paran en la estación de Baños únicament cuando está abierto el Balneario.

SANTAÑY A PALMA

PRECIOS 1.ª	2.ª	3.ª	K.	ESTACIONES	71 Cor. 1-2-3	73 Mix. 1-2	75 Mix. 1-2			
P. C.	P. C.	P. C.								
»	»	»	»	SANTAÑY.................... S..	6.40	12.10	17.20	—	—	—
0,45	0,30	0,20	7	Las Salinas....................	6.51	12.21	17.35	—	—	—
0,75	0,45	0,25	10	Baños de San Juan....................	6.58	12.27	17.41	—	—	—
1,00	0,80	0,45	18	Campos....................	7.13	12.47	18. 1	—	—	—
2,00	1,35	0,65	32	Lluchmayor....................	7.52	13.31	18.29	—	—	—
3,05	2,00	1,00	40	El Arena....................	8.23	14. 1	18.52	—	—	—
3,60	2,35	1,25	50	Coll d'en Rebassa....................	8.38	14.16	19. 3	—	—	—
4,00	2,60	1,40	62	*PALMA....................	8.50	14.25	19.13	—	—	—

TREN 73.—Circula los jueves.

CONSELL A ALAROS

Entre estos dos puntos hay un tranvía de 4 kilometros de extensión, por el que circulan trenes ascendentes y descendentes en combinación con la línea de Palma a Manacor y cuyos asientos cuestan 30 y 20 centimos según sean de 1.ª ó 2.ª clase

Km.	ESTACIONES		4 Cor.	6 Cor.	8 Trn.	12-84 Cor.	14-84 Cor.	16 Lig.	16 bis Lig. ⊕✝	10-54 Cor.	Cor.	6-62 Cor.	16-56 Lig.	16-66 Lig.				
—	● PALMA	S.	8.00	8.40	13.25	14.15	14.45	18.30	21.80	—	—	—	—	—				
4	Pont d'Inca	S.	8.09		13.35		14.54	18.39	21.09	—	—	—	—	—				
9	Marratxi	S.	8.20	8.57	13.49		15.05	18.50	21.20	—	—	—	—	—				
15	● SANTA MARIA	Ll.	8.37	9.12	14.05		15.19	19.06	21.36	—	—							
—	● SANTA MARIA	S.								15.06	—		19.33	—				
7	SANTA EUGENIA	S.								15.20	—		19.48	—				
16	ALGAIDA	S.								15.41	—		20.11	—				
23	MONTUIRI	S.								15.54	—		20.28	—				
26	PORRERAS	S.								16.03	—		20.48	—				
30	LAS CANTERAS	S.								16.25	—		20.57	—				
43	FELANITX	Ll.								16.40	—		21.12	—				
—	● SANTA MARIA	S.	8.37	9.12	14.05		15.19	19.06	21.36	—	—							
19	Consell	S.		9.20	14.15		15.28	19.15		—	—							
22	Binisalem	S.		9.28	14.25		15.37	19.24	21.45	—	—							
26	Lloseta	S.	8.45	9.36			15.46	19.34	22.04	—	—							
29	Inca	S.	9.03	9.46	14.34		15.58	19.50	22.11	—	—							
34	● EMPALME	Ll.	9.15	9.54	14.42	15.10	16.06	20.05	22.35	—	—							
—	● EMPALME	S.			—		—	—	—	—	—	9.55	16.08	20.03				
5	LLUBI	S.			—		—	—	—	—	—	10.06	16.20	20.18				
9	MURO	S.			—		—	—	—	—	—	10.16	16.32	20.33				
13	LA PUEBLA	Ll.			—		—	—	—	—	—	10.25	16.41	20.42				
—	● EMPALME	S.	9.15	—	—	15,10	—	20.05	22.35	—	—							
4	Sineu	S.	9.40	—	—		—	20.19	22.49	—	—							
5	San Juan	S.	9.46	—	—	15.36	—	20.25	22.55	—	—							
4	Petra	S.	9.43	—	—	15.42	—	20.40	23.10	—	—							
4	MANACOR	Ll.}S.	10.02	—	—	15.58	—	20.56	23.16	—	—							
			10.27	—	—	16.23	—			—	—							
3	San Lorenzo	S.	10.46	—	—	16.42	—	—	—	—	—							
7	San Miguel	S.	10.56	—	—	16.49	—	—	—	—	—							
84	San Servera	S.	11.14	—	—	17.04	—	—	—	—	—							
94	ARTA	Ll.	11.30	—	—	17.20	—	—	—	—	—							

El tren 16-66 retrasa su salida los domingos hasta las 20.—. Los trenes 16-66 y 68-11 son discrecionales.—El tren 16 retrasa su salida los sábados hasta las 19,50, y los festivos hasta las 20,50.

E.F.E.   1954

Km.	ESTACIONES		1 Trn.	61-3 Cor.	81-5 Cor.	11 Lig.	13 Trn. ⊕⊕	83-15 Cor.	15 bis ✝	51-3 Cor.	53-11 Lig.	55-17 Cor.	63-11 Mix.	65-15 Cor.			
—	ARTA	Ll.	—	—	6.35	—	—	16.00	—	—	—	—	—	—			
10	San Servera	S.	—	—	6.50	—	—	16.19	—	—	—	—	—	—			
17	San Miguel	S.	—	—	7.02	—	—	16.35	—	—	—	—	—	—			
21	San Lorenzo	S.	—	—	7.09	—	—	16.47	—	—	—	—	—	—			
30	MANACOR	Ll.}S.	5.05	—	7.30	—	—	17.12	—	—	—	—	—	—			
40	Petra	S.	5.22	—	7.50	—	—	17.32	—	—	—	—	—	—			
49	San Juan	S.	5.37	—	8.05	—	—	17.48	—	—	—	—	—	—			
51	Sineu	S.	5.44	—	—	—	—	17.59	—	—	—	—	—	—			
60	● EMPALME	S.	6.00	—	8.14	—	—	18.23	—	—	—	—	—	—			
—	LA PUEBLA	Ll.		7.00		—		—		—	—	12.10	17.33	—			
4	MURO	S.		7.13		—		—		—	—	12.23	17.47	—			
8	LLUBI	S.		7.25		—		—		—	—	12.38	18.04	—			
13	● EMPALME	Ll.		7.35		—		—		—	—	12.48	18.16	—			
60	● EMPALME	Ll.	6.00	7.36		12.51	—	18.23	21.00	—	—	—	—	—			
65	Inca	S.	6.15	7.55	8.41	13.04	17.00	18.38	21.07	—	—	—	—	—			
68	Lloseta	S.	6.23	8.05		13.12	17.07	18.46	21.14	—	—	—	—	—			
72	Binisalem	S.	6.31	8.15	8.54	13.21	17.14	18.55	21.21	—	—	—	—	—			
75	Consell	S.	6.39	8.25		13.28	17.21	19.03	21.21	—	—	—	—	—			
79	● SANTA MARIA	S.	6.47	8.35	9.08	13.39	17.28	19.12	21.28	—	—	—	—	—			
—	FELANITX	Ll.								7.00	—	17.20	—	—			
7	LAS CANTERAS	S.								7.12	—	17.32	—	—			
13	PORRERAS	S.								7.27	—	17.50	—	—			
20	MONTUIRI	S.								7.44	—	18.09	—	—			
27	ALGAIDA	S.								8.01	—	18.26	—	—			
36	SANTA EUGENIA	S.								8.16	—	18.41	—	—			
43	SANTA MARIA	S.								8.35	—	18.54	—	—			
79	● SANTA MARIA	Ll.	6.47	8.35	9.08	13.39	17.28	18.48	21.28				—	—			
85	Marratxi	S.	6.57	8.45	9.18	13.49	17.47	19.22	21.47				—	—			
90	Pont d'Inca	S.	7.06	8.54	9.27	13.58	17.47	19.31	21.47				—	—			
94	● PALMA	Ll.	7.14	9.02	9.35	14.05	17.55	19.39	21.55				—	—			

502   PALMA A ARTA   502
(SERVICIO DESDE EL 1.º DE ABRIL DE 1959)

		K.	ESTACIONES	132 Auto	82 Auto	134 Auto	104 Auto	118 Cor.	84 Cor.	66 Mix.	138 Auto	112 Auto	66 bis Lig.	112 Auto
25	I		.PALMA ..... S.	8.—	9.—	12.30	13.25	14.25	14.45	18.60	19.10	20.10	20.30	22.—
	D	4	Pont	8.06	9.05	12.35	13.30	»	14.54	18.39		20.16	20.39	22.06
	D	9	Marratxi	8.11	9.10	12.41	13.38	»	15.05	»		»	»	»
	D	15	*SANTA MARIA	8.19	9.18	12.49	13.49	»	15.19	19.03		20.29	21.03	22.19
153	I	19	Consell	8.26	9.24	12.55	13.55	»	15.28	19.11		20.35	21.11	22.25
	D	22	Biniasem	8.31	9.30	13.—	14.01	»	15.37	19.19		20.41	21.19	22.31
	I	26	Lloseta	8.37	9.36	13.05	14.07	»	15.46	19.27		20.47	21.27	22.37
	I	29	Inca	8.44	9.43	13.10	14.12	15.10	15.58	19.37	19.48	20.53	21.37	22.48
88	I	34	*EMPALME		9.49				16.06	19.48		20.59	21.48	22.49
	D	43	Sineu	9.02		13.25		16.36			20.05	21.10		23.—
	D	46	San Juan	9.06		13.28		16.42			20.08	21.13		23.08
	D	54	Petra	9.17		13.38		16.58			0.19	21.24		23.14
73	D	64	Manacor	9.30		13.51		16.23			.31	21.35		23.25
	D	73	San Lorenzo ...	9.42		14.03		16.42			20.43			
	D	77	San Miguel	9.47		14.08		16.49			20.48			
	I	84	S. Servera	9.57		14.18		17.04			20.58			
116	D	94	ARTA .... Ll.	10.08		14.19		17.20			21.09			

		K.	ESTACIONES	111 Auto	61 Cor.	121 Auto	63 Auto	133 Auto	103 Tran.	85 Cor.	135 Auto	137 Lig.
116	I		ARTA ..... S.			7.55		13.12			17.50	18.50
	D	10	S. Servera			8.07		13.24			18.04	19.05
	I	17	San Miguel			8.17		13.84			18.12	19.17
		21	San Lorenzo ...			8.22		13.39			18.17	19.24
73	I	30	Manacor	6.—		8.35		13.56			18.29	19.41
	I	40	Petra	6.13		8.47		14.08			18.41	19.58
	I	49	San Juan	6.24		8.58		14.17			18.52	20.14
	I	51	Sineu	6.30		9.08		14.21			18.56	20.21
88	D	60	*EMPALME	6.42	7.35	9.12	12.55	»		18.23	»	20.37
	O	65	Inca	6.50	7.53	9.21	13.08	14.36	17.—	18.38	19.13	21.
	D	68	Lloseta	6.56	8.01	»	13.05	14.41	17.06	18.46	»	21.07
	I	72	Biniasem	7.02	8.09	9.32	13.16	14.46	17.12	18.55	19.24	21.14
153	I	75	Consell	7.08	8.17		13.21	14.51	17.18	19.03	»	21.21
	I	79	*SANTA MARIA	7.14	8.25	9.43	13.27	14.57	17.24	19.12	19.35	21.28
	I	85	Marratxi	7.23	8.35	»	13.34	15.06	17.33	19.23	»	21.38
	I	90	Pont	7.30	8.44	9.56	13.39	15.11	17.40	19.31	19.48	21.47
25	D	94	*PALMA .... Ll.	7.36	8.52	10.01	13.44	15.15	17.45	19.39	19.53	21.55

El tren 138 circula los festivos una hora después.

503   PALMA A FELANITX   503
(SERVICIO DESDE EL 1.º DE ABRIL DE 1959)

	K.	ESTACIONES	54 Auto	58 Auto	K.	ESTACIONES	51 Auto	55 Auto
I		*PALMA ..... S.	14.15	19.15		FELANITX .... S.	7.30	17.30
D	15	*SANTA MARIA	14.39	19.39	7	Cantera	7.39	17.39
D	22	Santa Eugenia	14.49	19.49	13	Porreras	7.51	17.51
D	31	Algaida (155 m.) ..	15.03	20.03	20	Montuiri	8.04	18.04
I	38	Montuiri	15.13	20.13	27	Algaida	8.16	18.16
I	45	Porreras	15.26	20.26	36	Santa Eugenia	8.29	18.29
D	51	Cantera	15.37	20.37	43	*SANTA MARIA	8.39	18.39
D	58	FELANITX (90 m.) Ll	15.46	20.46	58	*PALMA Ll	9,—	19.—

El trayecto detallado entre Palma y Santa Maria y viceversa, véase en el itinerario 502.
Los trenes 55 y 56 retrasan una hora su salida los dias festivos del 1.º de octubre al 31 de mayo, y después dos horas.

504   PALMA A LA PUEBLA   504
(SERVICIO DESDE EL 1.º DE ABRIL DE 1959)

		K.	ESTACIONES	62 Auto	64 Cor.	L 66 Lig.		ESTACIONES	61 Cor.	63 Auto	65 Cor.
24			*PALMA ..... S.	9.—	14.45	18.30		LA PUEBLA ..... S.	7.—	12.30	17.33
	I	34	*EMPALME .... { Ll	9.47	16.06	19.43		Muro	7.13	12.38	17.47
			{ S.	9.49	16.08	19.48		Llubí	7.24	12.47	18.04
6	D	39	Llubí	9.58	16.30	20.03	13	*EMPALME ... { Ll	7.34	12.15	18.16
	D	44	Muro	10.07	16.32	20.18		{ S.	7.36	12.55	18.26
18	I	47	LA PUEBLA .. Ll	10.14	16.41	20.27	47	*PALMA Ll	8.52	13.44	19.29

El tren 66 retrasa su salida los festivos hasta las 20.30.
El trayecto detallado entre Palma y Empalme y viceversa, véase en el itinerario 502.

505   PALMA A SANTAÑY   505
(SERVICIO DESDE EL 1.º DE ABRIL DE 1959)

Alt.		K.	ESTACIONES	72 Auto	74 Auto	76 Auto	78 Auto	K.	ESTACIONES	71 Auto	73 Auto	75 Auto	75 Auto
5	I	1	*PALMA ... S.	9 20	14 30	19 20	20 20		SANTAÑY S.	7 30	12 45	17 30	18 30
9	D	6	Coll	9 28	14 38	19 28	20 28	4	Llomparts (ap.) ..	7 34	12 49	17 34	18 34
	I	11	San Francisco. ...	9 34	14 44	19 34	20 34	7	Salinas	7 39	12 54	17 39	18 49
	D	14	Arenal	9 40	14 50	19 40	20 40	10	Baños	7 44	12 59	17 44	18 44
136	I	30	Lluchmayor	10 01	15 11	20 01	2 01	18	Campos	7 54	13 09	17 54	18 54
	I	44	Campos	10 17	15 27	20 17	21 17	32	Lluchmayor	8 03	13 28	18 12	19 13
	D	52	Baños	10 26	15 36	20 26	21 26	48	Arenal	8 31	13 46	18 41	19 31
	D	55	Salinas	10 32	15 42	20 32	21 32	51	San Francisco. ..	8 36	13 51	18 36	19 36
	D	58	Llomparts (ap.) ..	10 36	15 46	20 36	21 36	56	Coll	8 43	13 59	18 43	19 43
	D	62	SANTAÑY Ll	10 41	15 50	20 40	21 40	62	*PALMA .. Ll.	8 50	14 05	18 50	19 50

Del 1.º junio al 30 septiembre los trenes 75 y 76 circulan los dias festivos dos horas más tarde que los laborables.

Km.	ESTACIONES 1-VII-960	132 Aut.	134	104 A Aut.	136 Aut.	138	138 bis	112 Aut.	112 bis Aut.		
						✠	✠	✠	✠		
0	**Palma** .... S.	8.—	12.30	13.25	15.30	19.10	20.10	20.10	22.—		
4	Pont	8.06	12.37	13.30				20.16	22.06		
9	Marratxi	8.11	12.44	13.38							
15	**Santa María**	8.19	12.55	13.49		19.34	20.34	20.29	22.19		
19	Consell	8.25	13.01	13.55		19.40	20.40	20.35	22.25		
22	Biniamen	8.31	13.07	14.01	15.58	19.46	20.46	20.41	22.31		
26	Lloseta	8.37	13.13	14.07	16.04	19.52	20.52	20.47	22.37		
29	Inca	8.44	13.19	14.12	16.10	19.58	20.58	20.53	22.43		
34	**Empalme**	8.50	13.25			20.04	21.04	20.59	22.49		
43	Sineu	9.02	13.36		16.27	20.15	21.15	21.10	23.—		
46	San Juan	9.06	13.40		16.31	20.20	21.20	21.13	23.03		
54	Petra	9.17	13.52		16.42	20.31	21.31	21.24	23.14		
64	Manacor	9.30	14.04		16.55	20.43	21.43	21.35	23.25		
78	San Lorenzo	9.42	14.16		17.07	20.55	21.55				
77	San Miguel	9.47	14.22		17.12	21.01	22.01				
84	S. Servera	9.57	14.33		17.22	21.12	22.12				
94	**Artá** .... Ll.	10.08	14.45		17.33	21.24	22.24				

Km.	ESTACIONES	111 Aut.	131	133 Aut.	135	137 Aut.	103 A Aut.				
							✠				
0	**Artá** .... S.		7.15	13.—	16.10	17.50					
10	S. Servera		7.28	13.12	16.23	18.02					
17	San Miguel		7.39	13.22	16.34	18.12					
21	San Lorenzo		7.45	13.27	16.40	18.17					
30	Manacor	6.—	7.58	13.39	16.54	18.29					
40	Petra	6.13	8.10	13.52	17.06	18.41					
49	San Juan	6.24	8.21	14.03	17.17	18.52					
51	Sineu	6.30	8.26	14.07	17.22	18.56					
60	**Empalme**	6.42		14.17	17.32	19.06					
65	Inca	6.50	8.44	14.24	17.39	19.13	21.—				
68	Lloseta	6.56	8.50	14.30	17.45	19.19	21.06				
72	Biniamen	7.02	8.56	14.36	17.51	19.25	21.12				
75	Consell	7.08		14.42	17.57	19.31	21.18				
79	**Santa María**	7.14	9.07	14.48	18.03	19.37	21.24				
85	Marratxi	7.23		14.56	18.11	19.44	21.33				
90	Pont	7.30	9.22	15.02	18.18	19.50	21.40				
94	**Palma** .... Ll.	7.35	9.28	15.07	18.24	19.55	21.45				

A Circula ⑧ ⑩ ✠ y vísperas de ✠

---

215   Palma - Felanitx   **215**

Km.	ESTACIONES 1-VII-960	52 Aut.	54 Aut.	66 Aut.	Km.	ESTACIONES 1-VII-960	51 Aut.	53 Aut.	55 Aut.
				A					A
0	**Palma** .... S.	9.25	14.15	19.15	0	**Felanitx** .... S.	7.30	12.30	17.30
15	**Santa María** ...	9.49	14.39	19.39	7	Cas Concos	7.39	12.39	17.39
23	Santa Eugenia	9.59	14.49	19.49	13	Porreras	7.51	12.51	17.51
31	Algaida	10.13	15.03	20.03	20	Montuiri	8.04	13.04	18.04
38	Montuiri	10.23	15.13	20.13	27	Algaida	8.16	13.16	18.16
45	Porreras	10.36	15.26	20.26	36	Santa Eugenia	8.29	13.29	18.29
54	Cas Concos	10.47	15.37	20.37	43	**Santa María**	8.39	13.39	18.39
65	**Felanitx** .... Ll.	10.56	15.46	20.46	58	**Palma** .... Ll.	9.—	13.59	19.—

A Retrasan una hora su salida los días festivos, del 1-X al 31-V, y dos horas, del 1-VI al 30-IX.

---

216   Palma - La Puebla   **216**

Km.	ESTACIONES 1-VII-960	62 Aut.	64 Aut.	66 Aut.	68 Aut.	68 bis Aut.	Km.	ESTACIONES 1-VII-960	61 Aut.	63 Aut.	65 Aut.	67 Aut.
						✠						
0	**Palma** .... S.	9.—	12.10	15.—	18.50	20.30	0	**La Puebla** .. S.	7.30	10.20	13.30	17.30
	Empalme . Ll.	9.47	12.56	15.46	19.36	21.17						
34	**Empalme** . S.	9.49	12.58	15.48	19.38	21.19	4	Muro	7.38	10.28	13.38	17.38
39	Llubí	9.58	13.07	15.57	19.47	21.28	8	Llubí	7.47	10.37	13.47	17.47
43	Muro	10.07	13.16	16.06	19.56	21.37		**Empalme** — Ll.	7.52	10.44	13.54	17.53
47	**La Puebla** .. Ll.	10.14	13.23	16.13	20.03	21.44	13	**Empalme** — S.	7.55	10.46	13.56	17.56
							47	**Palma** .... Ll.	8.44	11.33	14.43	18.43

---

213   Palma-Santañy   **213**

Km.	72 Aut.	74 Aut.	76 Aut.	ESTACIONES (1-VII-960)	71 Aut.	73 Aut.	75 Aut.
			A				A
0	9.20	14.30	19.20	S. **Palma** .... Ll.	8.50	14.05	18.50
6	9.28	14.38	19.28	Coll	8.43	13.58	18.43
11	9.34	14.44	19.34	San Francisco (apd.) .	8.36	13.51	18.36
12	9.37	14.47	19.37	Las Cadenas (apd.) ..	8.33	13.48	18.33
14	9.40	14.50	19.40	Arenal	8.31	13.46	18.31
30	10.01	15.11	20.01	Lluchmayor	8.13	13.28	18.13
34	10.17	15.27	20.17	Campos	7.54	13.09	17.54
48	10.23	15.33	20.23	El Palmer (apd.)	7.47	13.02	17.47
52	10.26	15.36	20.26	Baños	7.44	12.59	17.44
56	10.32	15.42	20.32	Salinas	7.39	12.54	17.39
62	10.36	15.46	20.36	Llombarts (apd.)	7.34	12.49	17.34
68	10.40	15.50	20.40	Ll. **Santañy** ...... S.	7.30	12.45	17.30

A Retrasan su salida una hora los ✠, del 1-X al 31-V, y dos horas, del 1-VI al 30-IX.

Km.	ESTACIONES	132 Aut.	102	134	104 Aut.	136 Aut.	138	106 Aut.	138 bis	112 Aut.	112 bis Aut.
0	PALMA .... S.	8.—	10.—	12.30	14.—	15.30	19.10	19.30	20.10	20.10	22.—
4	Pont.	8.06	10.05	12.37	14.05			19.35		20.16	22.06
9	Marratxi	8.11	10.13	12.44	14.13			19.43			
15	Santa María	8.19	10.24	12.55	14.24		19.34	19.54	20.34	20.29	22.19
19	Consell	8.25	10.30	13.01	14.30		19.40	20.—	20.40	20.35	22.25
22	Binisalem	8.31	10.36	13.07	14.36	15.58	19.46	20.06	20.46	20.41	22.31
26	Lloseta	8.37	10.42	13.13	14.42	16.04	19.52	20.12	20.52	20.47	22.37
29	Inca	8.44	10.47	13.19	14.47	16.10	19.58	20.17	20.58	20.53	22.43
34	Empalme	8.50	—	13.25	—		20.04	—	21.04	20.59	22.49
43	Sineu	9.02	—	13.36	—	16.27	20.15	—	21.15	21.10	23.—
45	San Juan	9.06	—	13.40	—	16.31	20.20	—	21.20	21.13	23.03
54	Petra	9.17	—	13.52	—	16.42	20.31	—	21.31	21.24	23.14
64	Manacor	9.30	—	14.04	—	16.55	20.43	—	21.43	21.35	23.25
73	San Lorenzo	9.42	—	14.16	—	17.07	20.55	—	21.55	—	—
77	San Miguel	9.47	—	14.22	—	17.12	21.01	—	22.01	—	—
84	Son Servera	9.57	—	14.33	—	17.22	21.12	—	22.12	—	—
94	ARTA .... Ll.	10.08	—	14.45	—	17.33	21.24	—	22.24	—	—

473   Artá ⟶ Palma

Km.	ESTACIONES	111 Aut.	131	101 Aut.	133 Aut.	103 Aut.	135	137 bis Aut.	105 Aut.	137 Aut.
0	ARTA .... S.	—	7.15	—	13.—	—	16.10	18.20	—	17.50
10	Son Servera	—	7.28	—	13.12	—	16.23	18.34	—	18.02
17	San Miguel	—	7.39	—	13.22	—	16.34	18.46	—	18.12
21	San Lorenzo	—	7.45	—	13.27	—	16.40	18.52	—	18.17
30	Manacor	6.—	7.58	—	13.39	—	16.54	19.05	—	18.29
40	Petra	6.13	8.10	—	13.52	—	17.06	19.19	—	18.41
49	San Juan	6.24	8.21	—	14.03	—	17.17	19.32	—	18.52
51	Sineu	6.30	8.26	—	14.07	—	17.22	19.39	—	18.56
60	Empalme	6.42		—	14.17	—	17.32	19.51	—	19.06
65	Inca	6.50	8.44	—	14.24	16.30	17.39	19.58	21.—	19.13
68	Lloseta	6.56	8.50	13.06	14.30	16.36	17.45	20.05	21.06	19.19
72	Binisalem	7.02	8.56	13.12	14.36	16.42	17.51	20.12	21.12	19.25
75	Consell	7.08		13.18	14.42	16.48	17.57	20.18	21.18	19.31
79	Santa María	7.14	9.07	13.24	14.48	16.54	18.03	20.24	21.24	19.37
85	Marratxi	7.23		13.33	14.56	17.03	18.11	20.32	21.33	19.44
90	Pont.	7.30	9.22	13.40	15.02	17.10	18.18	20.39	21.40	19.50
94	PALMA .... Ll.	7.35	9.28	13.45	15.07	17.15	18.24	20.50	21.45	19.55

474   Palma ⟷ Felanitx ⟷ Palma

Km.	52 Aut.	54 Aut.	56 Aut. A	ESTACIONES	51 Aut.	53 Aut.	55 Aut. A
0	9.25	14.15	19.15	S. PALMA Ll.	9.—	13.59	19.—
4		14.20	19.20	Pont d'Inca	8.55	13.54	18.55
9		14.28	19.28	Marratxi	8.48	13.47	18.48
15	9.49	14.39	19.39	Santa María	8.39	13.38	18.39
22	9.59	14.49	19.49	Santa Eugenia	8.29	13.28	18.29
31	10.13	15.03	20.03	Algaida	8.16	13.16	18.16
38	10.23	15.13	20.13	Montuiri	8.04	13.04	18.04
45	10.36	15.26	20.26	Porreras	7.51	12.51	17.51
51	10.47	15.37	20.37	Canteras	7.39	12.39	17.39
58	10.56	15.46	20.46	Ll. FELANITX S.	7.30	12.30	17.30

A. Del 1-X al 31-V, retrasan una hora su salida.

Palma ⟷ La Puebla ⟷ Palma   475

Km.	62 Aut.	64 Aut.	66 Aut.	68 Aut.	68 bis Aut.	ESTACIONES	61 Aut.	63 Aut.	65 Aut.	67 Aut.
0	9.—	12.10	15.—	18.50	20.30	S. PALMA Ll.	8.44	11.33	14.43	18.43
4	9.05	12.15	15.05	18.55	20.35	Pont d'Inca	8.39	11.28	14.38	18.38
9	9.10	12.20	15.10	19.—	20.40	Marratxi	8.34	11.23	14.33	18.33
15	9.18	12.28	15.18	19.08	20.48	Santa María	8.27	11.16	14.26	18.26
19	9.24	12.34	15.24	19.14	20.54	Consell	8.21	11.10	14.20	18.20
22	9.30	12.40	15.30	19.20	21.—	Binisalem	8.15	11.04	14.14	18.14
26	9.36	12.46	15.36	19.26	21.06	Lloseta	8.09	10.58	14.08	18.08
29	9.43	12.52	15.42	19.32	21.13	Inca	8.03	10.52	14.02	18.02
34	9.49	12.58	15.48	19.38	21.19	Empalme	7.55	10.45	13.55	17.55
39	9.58	13.07	15.57	19.47	21.28	Llubí	7.47	10.37	13.47	17.47
43	10.07	13.16	16.06	19.56	21.37	Muro	7.38	10.28	13.38	17.38
47	10.14	13.23	16.13	20.03	21.44	Ll. LA PUEBLA S	7.30	10.20	13.30	17.30

(3) Circula los sábados, domingos, festivos y vísperas.

F.E.V.E.

1972

PALMA - ARTA - PALMA

TREN 130	TREN 132	TREN 134	TREN 136	Kms.	ESTACIONES	Kms.	TREN 131	TREN 133	TREN 135	TREN 137
8,00	13,00	16,00	18,50	—	Palma	94	9,19	12,08	16,59	19,59
8,05	13,05	16,05	18,55	4	Pont d'Inca	90	9,14	12,03	16,54	19,54
8,10	13,10	16,10	19,00	9	Marratxi	85	9,09	11,58	16,49	19,49
8,18	13,18	16,18	19,08	15	Santa Maria	79	9,02	11,51	16,42	19,42
8,23	13,23	16,23	19,13	19	Consell	75	8,56	11,45	16,36	19,36
8,28	13,27	16,27	19,18	22	Binisalem	72	8,52	11,41	16,32	19,32
8,34	13,33	16,33	19,24	26	Lloseta	68	8,46	11,35	16,26	19,26
8,40	13,39	16,39	19'29	29	Inca	65	8,41	11,30	16,21	19,21
8,46	13,45	16,45	19,35	34	Empalme	60	8,33	11,23	16,14	19,14
8,56	13,55	16,55	19,46	43	Sineu	51	8,23	11,13	16,04	19,04
8,59	13,58	16,58	19,49	45	San Juan	49	8,20	11,10	16,01	19,01
9,11	14,10	17,10	20,01	54	Petra	40	8,09	10,59	15,50	18,50
9,23	14,22	17,22	20,13	64	Manacor	30	7,57	10,47	15,39	18,39
9,35	14,34	17,34	20,24	73	San Lorenzo	21	7,45	10,35	15,27	18,27
9,39	14,38	17,38	20,28	77	San Miguel	17	7,40	10,30	15,22	18,22
9,48	14,47	17,47	20,38	84	Son Servera	10	7,31	10,21	15,13	18,13
9,59	14,58	17,58	20,49	94	Artà	—	7,20	10,10	15,02	18,02

PALMA - LA PUEBLA - PALMA

TREN 160	TREN 162	TREN 164	TREN 166	Kms.	ESTACIONES	Kms.	TREN 161	TREN 163	TREN 165	TREN 167
9,00	12,00	15,00	19,20	—	Palma	47	8,33	11,33	14,18	18,48
9,05	12,05	15,05	19,25	4	Pont d'Inca	43	8,28	11,28	14,13	18,43
9,10	12,10	15,10	19,30	9	Marratxi	38	8,23	11,23	14,08	18,38
9,18	12,18	15,18	19,38	15	Santa Maria	32	8,16	11,16	14,01	18,31
9,23	12,23	15,23	19,43	19	Consell	28	8,10	11,10	13,55	18,25
9,28	12,28	15,28	19,48	22	Binisalem	25	8,06	11,06	13,51	18,21
9,34	12,34	15,34	19,54	26	Lloseta	21	8,00	11,00	13,45	18,15
9,39	12,39	15,39	19,59	29	Inca	18	7,55	10,55	13,40	18,10
9,45	12,45	15,45	20,05	34	Empalme	13	7,48	10,48	13,33	18,03
9,52	12,52	15,52	20,12	39	Llubi	8	7,40	10,40	13,25	17,55
10,00	13,00	16,00	20,20	43	Muro	4	7,32	10,32	13,17	17,47
10,06	13,06	16,06	20,26	47	La Puebla	—	7,25	10,25	13,10	17,40

PALMA - INCA

ESTACIONES	Kms	TREN 100	TREN 102 (1)	TREN 104 (2)	TREN 130	TREN 160	TREN 106	TREN 108	TREN 162	TREN 132	TREN 116	TREN 164	TREN 134	TREN 112	TREN 114	TREN 136	TREN 166	TREN 116
Palma	—	6,15	7,35	7,45	8,00	9,00	9,30	11,00	12,00	13,00	14,00	15,00	16,00	17,00	18,25	18,50	19,20	20,00
Pont d'Inca	4	6,20	7,40	7,50	8,05	9,05	9,35	11,05	12,05	13,05	14,05	15,05	16,05	17,05	18,30	18,55	19,25	20,05
Marratxi	9	6,25	7,45	7,55	8,10	9,10	9,40	11,10	12,10	13,10	14,10	15,10	16,10	17,10	18,35	19,00	19,30	20,10
Santa Maria	15	6,33	7,53	8,03	8,18	9,18	9,48	11,18	12,18	13,18	14,18	15,18	16,18	17,18	18,43	19,08	19,38	20,18
Consell	19	6,38	7,58	8,08	8,23	9,23	9,53	11,23	12,23	13,23	14,23	15,23	16,23	17,23	18,48	19,13	19,43	20,23
Binisalem	22	6,43	8,03	8,13	8,28	9,28	9,58	11,28	12,28	13,27	14,28	15,28	16,27	17,28	18,53	19,18	19,48	20,28
Lloseta	26	6,49	8,09	8,19	8,34	9,34	10,04	11,34	12,34	13,33	14,34	15,34	16,33	17,34	18,59	19,24	19,54	20,34
Inca	29	6,53	8,13	8,23	8,40	9,39	10,08	11,38	12,39	13,39	14,38	15,39	16,39	17,38	19,03	19,29	19,59	20,38

TRENES ASCENDENTES. — Circulan diariamente con las variantes (1), solo DIAS LABORABLES y (2), solo DOMINGOS Y FESTIVOS

INCA - PALMA

ESTACIONES	Kms	TREN 101	TREN 103 (1)	TREN 105 (2)	TREN 161	TREN 131	TREN 107	TREN 163	TREN 133	TREN 109	TREN 165	TREN 111	TREN 135	TREN 113	TREN 167	TREN 115	TREN 137	TREN 117
Inca	—	6,55	8,15	8,28	7,55	8,41	10,15	10,55	11,30	12,00	13,40	15,00	16,21	17,45	18,10	19,10	19,21	20,40
Lloseta	3	7,00	8,20	8,33	8,00	8,46	10,20	11,00	11,35	12,05	13,45	15,05	16,26	17,50	18,15	19,15	19,26	20,45
Binisalem	7	7,06	8,26	8,39	8,06	8,52	10,26	11,05	11,41	12,11	13,51	15,11	16,32	17,56	18,21	19,21	19,32	20,51
Consell	10	7,10	8,30	8,43	8,10	8,56	10,30	11,10	11,45	12,15	13,55	15,15	16,36	18,00	18,25	19,25	19,36	20,56
Santa Maria	14	7,16	8,36	8,49	8,16	9,02	10,36	11,16	11,51	12,21	14,01	15,21	16,42	18,06	18,31	19,31	19,42	21,01
Marratxi	20	7,23	8,43	8,56	8,23	9,09	10,43	11,23	11,58	12,28	14,08	15,28	16,49	18,13	18,38	19,38	19,49	21,08
Pont d'Inca	25	7,28	8,48	9,01	8,28	9,14	10,48	11,28	12,03	12,33	14,13	15,33	16,54	18,18	18,43	19,43	19,54	21,13
Palma	29	7,33	8,53	9,06	8,33	9,19	10,53	11,33	12,08	12,38	14,18	15,38	16,59	18,23	18,48	19,48	19,59	21,18

TRENES DESCENDENTES. — Circulan diariamente con las variantes (1), solo DIAS LABORABLES y (2), solo DOMINGOS Y FESTIVOS

APPENDIX IV

The Soller Railway's Rule Book

As with all railways the daily workings of the FC de Soller were governed by a comprehensive set of regulations, and in the main these corresponded with those set out in the Law of 23rd November 1877, governing the workings of Spanish railways in general. However, the Soller company split their rule-book into seven sections, all printed separately, which could be given to the various operating departments according to need. Apart from a set of General Rules, there were booklets entitled Track Maintenance and Safety, Traffic Movement Regulations, and those applying to Locomotive Crews, Train Crews, Stationmasters and Pointsmen. The rules were comprehensive and covered every aspect including the qualifications for recruits in the various departments, together with a detailed list of the duties to be performed by each grade of employee. A representative selection is given below.

The minimum age for work on the footplate or as a member of the train crew (Conductors and Brakemen) was twenty years of age, but while Drivers and Firemen had to be "of a robust and healthy constitution" the former also had to be of good conduct, be able to read and write and have a notion of arithmetic, as well as being able to undertake running repairs to the locomotive. A Conductor had to be able to read, write and have a good knowledge of the four rules of arithmetic. In addition he had to have at least one year's service with the railway (or provide suitable references) and undergo a medical examination. He would need to have mastered the General Rule Book as well as the regulations for Traffic Movement, footplate and train crews, and know the signals used on the line. In addition he would need to be able to send and receive telegrams. It was the practice to have more than one Conductor on a train, and in this case the oldest man was designated Jefe del Tren (Trainmaster) with control over the other Conductor(s) and Brakemen as well as the footplate crew - while the train was in motion. While stopped at stations responsibility passed to the local Stationmaster.

At either end of the line the Stationmaster at Palma or Soller had a long list to check before allowing a train to proceed. He had to ensure that the footplate men and train crew knew the full details and timings of their trip, that all the staff were wearing the correct uniform, maintained in a clean and smart condition, and that the Driver had the correct tools, lamps and signals (presumably flags or detonators - the rule does not specify). The Conductors had to be checked to see that they too had the necessary safety equipment, copies of the Rule Books and the correct paperwork for any freight consignments being carried by the train. The Stationmaster also had to inspect the train itself, to see that the rolling stock was in good condition, that the buffer heights matched and the vehicles were correctly coupled. When the departure time arrived the Stationmaster would ring the station bell twice, which the Jefe del Tren would answer with two toots on his horn (somewhat similar to the shunter's horns used in Britain, and on Mallorca used instead of a guards whistle). This musical start to each journey was the signal and acknowledgement of the passing of responsibility from one official to the other.

While all this had been going on the engine would have arrived from the shed, where it would have been coaled, watered, oiled and inspected. Approaching the carriages the engine would be brought to a halt five metres in front of the train, before being slowly brought into contact for coupling up. After this had been accomplished the continuous brake was tested - the minimum air pressure required being 6kg. The engine had to be coupled to the train at least ten minutes before the scheduled departure time, no doubt to allow enough time for the brake test to be completed. Extracts from the General Rules stated that the locomotive should always be run at the head of the train, except when performing shunting duties in the vicinity of stations, and no more than two working locomotives should haul a train unless authorised by the Ministry of Public Works. Depending on the number of engines, an equivalent number of "non-passenger vehicles" (presumably brake vans) had to be marshalled between the locomotive(s) and the carriages. The provision of a tail-end "non-passenger vehicle" was advised by the Regulations, but the company could omit this at its discretion. Possibly as an assistance to braking power, the Jefe del Tren's brake van was always to carry a load of 2000kg. If its payload weighed below this amount, then ballast was to be added to bring it up to the required total.

Once the train had departed various rules governed any unexpected stops along the way. If help was needed the Jefe del Tren was to send to the nearest station, either by detaching the engine (assuming that it was not itself out of action) or by sending a relay of messengers on foot. One of the Brakemen would probably start by carrying the message which would be passed on to platelayers or other trackside workers for onward transmission. The message might be sent by different means in the same direction, but help was not to be sought from two different directions simultaneously. If, under the instructions of the Jefe del Tren, the locomotive was permitted to leave the train between stations, or if the couplings broke leaving the carriages stranded, then the train's manual brakes had to be applied and a "stop signal" (presumably a detonator) placed on the track 500 metres beyond the train to warn the returning locomotive. These latter rules also applied if the locomotive was in danger of running out of water and had to run ahead "light engine" to the next available water supply. Backing the train to the previous water tank was not allowed. In the event of an accident blocking the line a message to this effect had to be sent to the nearest station on either side of the train, with a copy to the Traffic Manager describing the nature of the accident, what help was needed and whether anyone had suffered injury.

Along the way, the level crossing keepers were often recruited from among the wives of other trackside employees. When not working at the barriers under their control they were authorised to attend to their household duties, but were strictly forbidden to take their children with them when working alongside the railway.

Once a train arrived safely at its destination the train crew were to place themselves at the disposal of the Jefe del Tren in order to help unload any freight consignments and to assist the departing passengers. Only when these tasks were completed would the Jefe del Tren give the other staff permission to leave the station. Meanwhile he had to complete the paperwork relating to his freight consignments and ticket returns, and write up the train report, before turning all this over to the local Stationmaster. During this period the engine crew would have taken the locomotive to the shed where a final check would be made, any faults being recorded in the Depot Register. At the end of the shift the Fireman had to drop the fire, and empty the ash from the smoke-box, making sure to close the smoke-box door afterwards to prevent damage caused by cold air cooling the boiler too rapidly.

PALMA Á SOLLER

PRECIOS			K.	ESTACIONES	2	4	6
1.ªc.	2.ªc.	3.ªc.					
»	»	»	»	• PALMA .... S...	7.40	15.»	20.»
			5	Son Sardina	7.50	15.10	20.10
			15	Buñola	8.10	15.50	20.20
			28	SOLLER .... Ll..	8.45	15.55	21.5

					1	3	5
				SOLLER .... S....	5.30	9.30	18.»
»	»	»	13	Buñola	6. 5	10. 5	18.35
			22	Son Sardina	6.25	10.25	18.55
			28	• PALMA .... Ll..	6.35	10.35	19. 5

Además de estos trenes, los domingos y días festivos saldrán otros dos de Palma para Soller á las 11.30 y 15.30 y otros dos de Soller para Palma á las 13.15 y 18.30.

1913

HORARIO DE TRENES			
SECCION PALMA-SOLLER		SECCION SOLLER-PUERTO	
Salid. Sóller	Salid. Palma	Salid. Sóller	Salid. Puerto
5,45	7,—	5,—	5,20
8,15	9,30	7,—	6,30
10,45	12,—	8,5	7,30
13,30	15,—	9,—	8,30
17,15	19,30	10,—	9,30
		10,45	10,20
		12,5	11,30
		13,5	12,30
		14,—	13,30
		15,—	14,30
		16,5	15,30
		18,—	16,30
		19,—	17,30
		20,35	18,30
			19,30
			20,55

c.1930

212   Palma-Soller   212

Km.	2 Cor. 1-2	4 Trn. 1-2	6 Cor. 1-2	8 Trn. 1-2	8 bis Trn 1-2	ESTACIONES (1-IV-959)	1 Trn. 1-2	3 Cor. 1-2	5 Trn. 1-2	7 bis Dor. 1-2
0	8.—	13.—	15.30	20.—	20.30	S.. Palma Ll..	7.40	10.15	15.10	21 —
6	8.10	13.10	15.40	20.10	22.40	Son Sardina	7.31	10.08	15.01	21.31
11	8.18	13.18	15.49	20.19	22.49	Santa Maria	7.23	9.58	14.53	21.38
15	8.28	13.28	15.59	20.29	22.59	Buñola	7.16	9.51	14.46	21.46
32	8.55	13.55	16.25	20.55	23.25	Ll.. Sóller S..	6.45	9.20	14.15	22.—

1958

BIBLIOGRAPHY

M. Kalla Bishop	Mediteranean Island Railways (David and Charles)
Allen & Wheeler	Steam On The Sierra (Cleaver Hulme Press)
J.M. Valerio & E. de la Cruz	The Majorca and Soller Railways (Aldaba Ediciones)
N.S. Canellas	La Iarda Mallorquina (Conselleria de Treball y Transports, Palma)
J. Morley & K. Plant	Minor Railways and Tramways in Eastern Spain
Narrow Gauge Railway Soc.	The Narrow Gauge numbers 48, 104, 108
Railway Magazine	April 1936, November 1985
Modern Tramway	April 1985
Chemain de Fer Regionaux et Urbains	number 148 (1985)
Carril	September 1966
Continental Railway Journal	Autumn 1991
M. Maristany	Carrilets de Espana y Portugal (vol. 1)
INECO	Plan Director De Transports de las Islas Baleares 1981
F.C. de Mallorca	Annual Reports for 1877, 1880
T.E.I.P.	Annual Report for 1959
T.E.I.P.	Transformacion y Modernizacion de los Transportes Urbanos & Interurbanos de Palma de Mallorca. 1959
S' Union de S' Arenal	number 10
Sa Veu de Lluchmajor	numbers 30, 32, 45, 46, 63
Bartolome Font Obrador	Miscelaneo Historica del Caserio del Arenal
Diario de Mallorca	6th April 1984
Carles salmeron i Bosch	El Tren d' Olot (Generalitat de Catalunya)
Industrial Railway Society	Industrial Locomotives of Spain and Portugal
Industrial Railway Record	number 89 (June 1981)
M.J. Fox	Last Steam Locomotives of Spain & Portugal (Ian Allen)
C.T. Bidwell	The Balearic Islands
Encyclopaedica Britannica	
Jane's World Railways	

A NOTE ON THE LOCOMOTIVE DRAWINGS

Drawings have been prepared largely from photographic evidence, supplemented by certain known dimensions. They are therefore offered as 'general arrangement' drawings and should not be regarded as definitive in all details.

MAJORCA RAILWAYS NASMYTH WILSON 0-4-0T (REBUILT FORM)

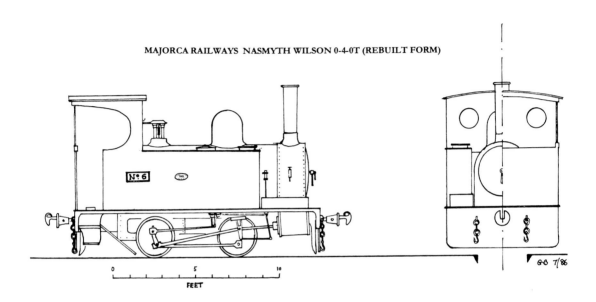

MAJORCA RAILWAYS NASMYTH WILSON 4-4-0T (REBUILT FORM)

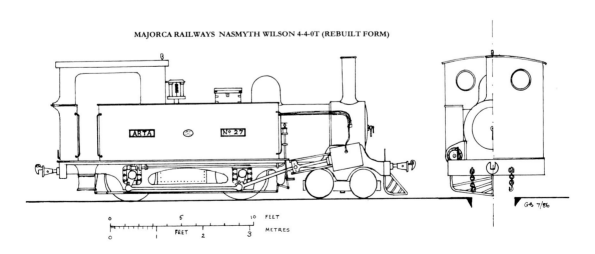

MAJORCA RAILWAYS NASMYTH WILSON 4-6-0T

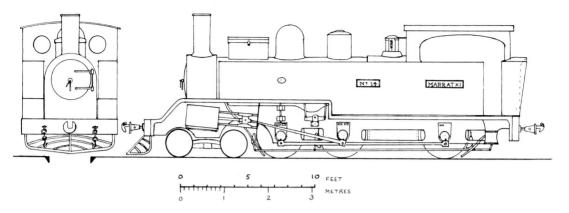

```
0          5          10  FEET
|____|____|____|____|  METRES
0      1      2      3
```

MAJORCA RAILWAYS B-B DIESEL LOCOMOTIVE

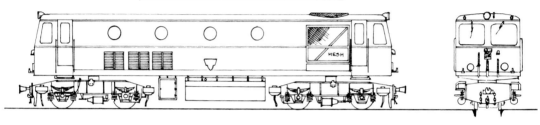

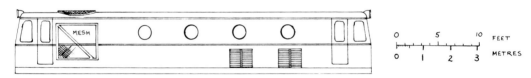

```
0          5          10  FEET
|____|____|____|  METRES
0      1      2      3
```

Drawn from photographs and dimensions taken from a similar locomotive on the Rio Tinto Railway

MAJORCA RAILWAYS MIXED CARRIAGE : 2nd & 3rd CLASS COMPARMENTS
Source: Maker's drawing (Brown Marshall) dated 1873

As drawn 1873   As running 1960   1873   1960

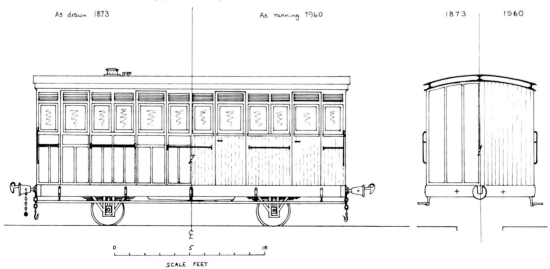

```
0          5          10
|____|____|____|
   SCALE FEET
```

MAJORCA RAILWAYS MIXED CARRIAGE WITH 2nd & 3rd CLASS ACCOMODATION PLUS GUARD'S COMPARMENT
Builder: Brown Marshall (1873) as running c. 1960

Notes

Original drawings show full panelling, although by 1960 matchboarding had been substituted.
At first brake wheel fitted in Guard's Comp^t but vac. brake added later and latterly out of use without hoses.

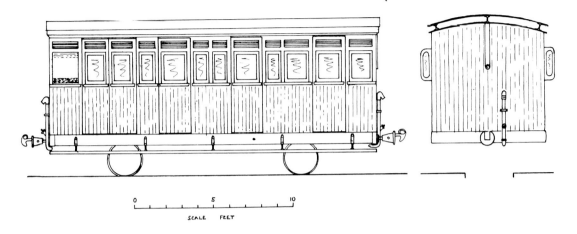

SCALE FEET
0   5   10

MAJORCA RAILWAYS BRAKE VAN (CLASS E)
Builder thought to be C A F Beasain. Drawn from photograph

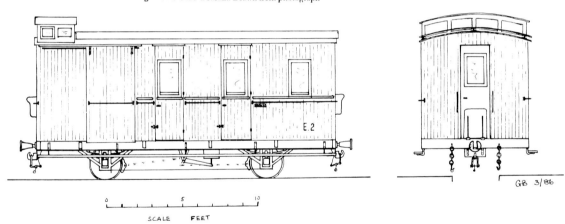

E.2

GB 3/86

SCALE FEET
0   5   10

MAJORCA RAILWAYS DROPSIDE OPEN WAGON (class B)
Builder C A F Beasain c. 1887 - c. 1917. Drawn from measurements taken in 1984.

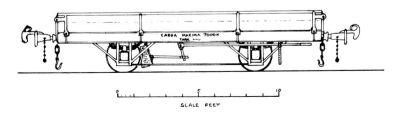

CARGA MAXIMA 7000K
TARA

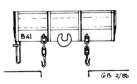

B 41

GB 2/86

SCALE FEET
0   5   10

MAJORCA RAILWAYS BRAKE VAN

Notes

It is not known whether this vehicle was a Brake Van with a Mail Compartment (as shown here with a post box at one end of the carriage) or a Brake/3rd. Another picture source shows two similar vehicles minus the post box and with an extra door (shown dotted).

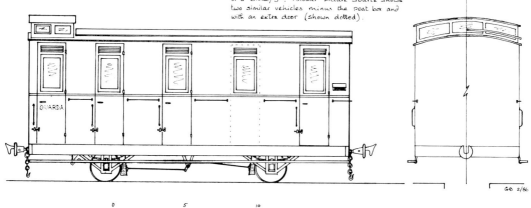

GB 2/86

SCALE FEET

MAJORCA RAILWAYS HIGH BODIED VENTILATED VAN (class C)

Builder thought to be C A F Beasain. Drawings based on photographs incorporating some known dimensions

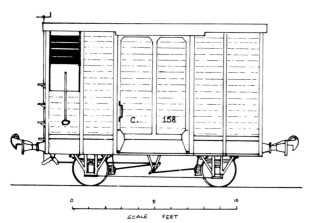

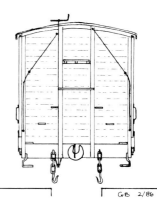

GB 2/86

SCALE FEET

MAJORCA RAILWAYS

DROPSIDE WAGON

Notes

① The brakesman's seat probably did not last long in use.
② Some examples had conventional solebar brake levers.

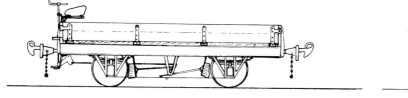

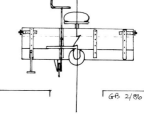

GB 2/86

SCALE FEET

MAJORCA RAILWAYS MIXED CARRIAGE : 2nd/3rd CLASS WITH GUARD'S BOX AND SCREW BRAKE

Builder: Brown Marshall. Drawn from maker's plans.

Notes

1873 : has Guards box, full panelling, door handles on the right of the doors. Class divisions: three 3rd cl. compartments, one 2nd cl.

1960 : Guard's box removed. Matchboard body. Door handles on the left. Class divisions: three 2nd class, one 1st class.

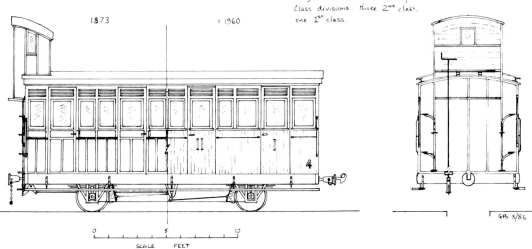

1873   c 1960

GB 3/86

0   5   10
SCALE   FEET

MAJORCA RAILWAYS HIGH SIDED OPEN WAGON (class A)
Source (Lower) Brown Marshall plans dated Dec 1873
(Upper) photographs c. 1960

Notes

The lower drawing shows the wagons as originally built. They obviously suffered during their working lives as subsequent alterations included large triangular plates (shown to the right of the doors) and extra transverse planking, marked ××, to reinforce the body. Some examples had brake levers at solebar level.

The upper drawing shows a variant with horizontal planking and L-shaped metal strapping, with triangular gussets. At least one wagon had some planks strengthened (marked ××).

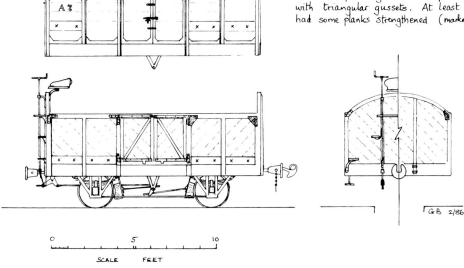

GB 2/86

0   5   10
SCALE   FEET

SOLLER RAILWAY

MOTOR COACH No. 1

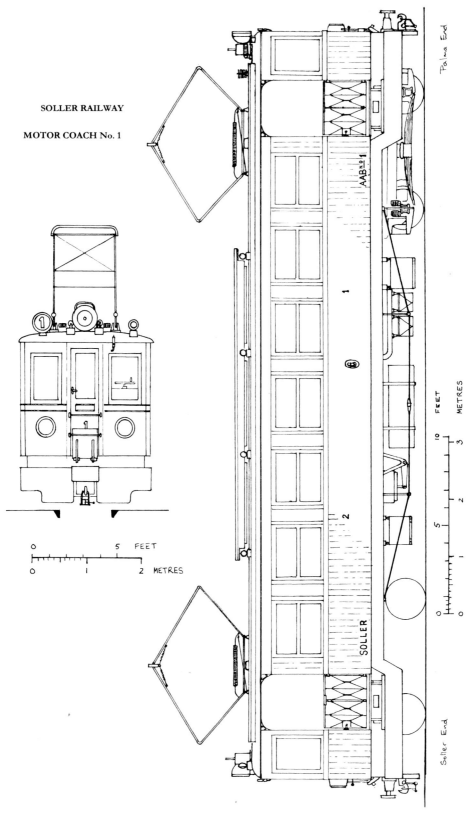

SOLLER RAILWAY COACH No. 8

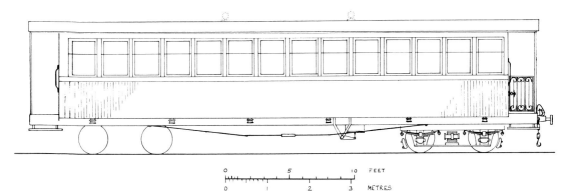

```
0              5              10    FEET
0        1          2          3    METRES
```

SOLLER RAILWAY BRAKE VAN No. F1

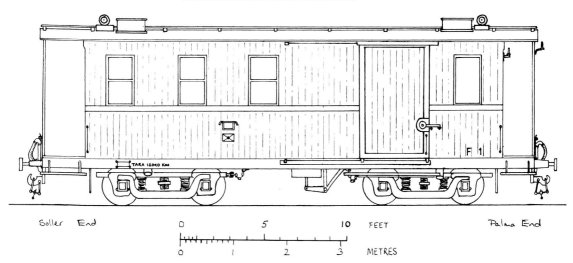

Soller End

Palma End

```
0              5              10    FEET
0        1          2          3    METRES
```

SOLLER RAILWAY GOODS VAN No. 8

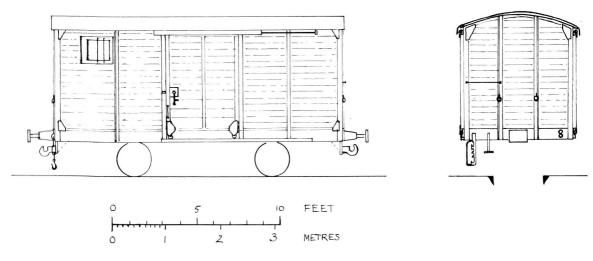

```
0              5              10    FEET
0        1          2          3    METRES
```

SOLLER RAILWAY DROPSIDE WAGON No. B1

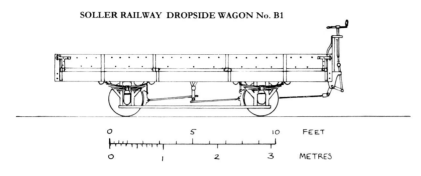
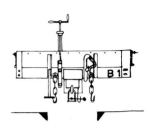

```
0          5          10    FEET
|-++++++|----+----|----+----|
0      1       2       3    METRES
```

SOLLER RAILWAY LOW-SIDED WAGON No. B9

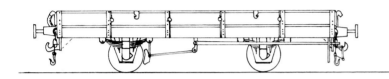
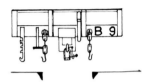

SOLLER RAILWAY BALCONY AND END DETAILS OF COACHES AND BRAKE VANS

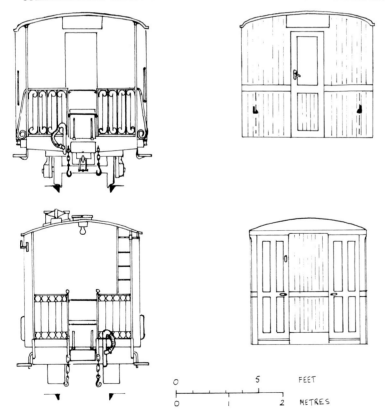

```
0              5        FEET
|----+----|----+----|
0        1         2   METRES
```